THE POLITICAL PRINCIPLES OF SOME NOTABLE

PRIME MINISTERS

OF THE

NINETEENTH CENTURY

THE POLITICAL PRINCIPLES OF SOME NOTABLE

PRIME MINISTERS

OF THE

NINETEENTH CENTURY

A SERIES OF LECTURES DELIVERED IN
KING'S COLLEGE, UNIVERSITY OF LONDON

EDITED BY

FOSSEY JOHN COBB HEARNSHAW

Essay Index Reprint Series

originally published by

MACMILLAN AND CO., LIMITED

 BOOKS FOR LIBRARIES PRESS

FREEPORT, NEW YORK

First Published 1926
Reprinted 1970

STANDARD BOOK NUMBER:

8369-1512-7

LIBRARY OF CONGRESS CATALOG CARD NUMBER:

74-107710

PRINTED IN THE UNITED STATES OF AMERICA

INTRODUCTORY NOTE

THE series of eight lectures contained in this volume was delivered in King's College, London, during the Spring Term of 1926. It enjoyed a wide popularity and attracted larger audiences than any similar course ever given at the College. Eminent chairmen consented to preside over the lectures, viz. Lord Hambleden, the Right Hon. L. C. M. S. Amery, Lord Peel, the Right Hon. Wilfrid Ashley, Lord Ampthill, Major Coningsby Disraeli, the Earl of Oxford, and the Lord Chancellor, Viscount Cave. Frequent requests were made during the process of the series that it might be made available in book form. The lecturers, several of whom had spoken merely from notes, were good enough to accede to the request for manuscript. The result is the present volume. It will be found that the different lecturers have interpreted the expression "political principles" very variously. It is hoped, however, that the variety of their interpretations will increase the interest of the book without unduly detracting from its value.

THE EDITOR.

KING'S COLLEGE, LONDON,
May 27, 1926.

CONTENTS

LECTURE I

LECTURE II

LECTURE III

LECTURE IV

GEORGE CANNING

By H. W. V. TEMPERLEY

I

IT seems to me appropriate that this series should
begin with Canning and with Wellington, two
opposed and contrasted types of men. My study
will endeavour to avoid political principles in their
technical sense. Canning, indeed, is remarkable
as being the subtlest and most intellectual of these
political thinkers, who have also been sufficiently
practical to lead the House of Commons or to head
the Government. But he is, in reality, more important than that, for he was in himself a political
principle. "The man", wrote Metternich, his
great rival in Europe, "was a revolution in himself alone ". And—years after Canning's death—
he wrote again, "The ministry of Mr. Canning
marked an era in the history of England and
Europe ".[1] Now that short premiership, "the

[1] Metternich to Esterhazy (London), August 12, 1831, *Vienna State
Archives,* quoted in my *Foreign Policy of Canning* (1925), p. 607. The
context proves that Metternich means by "ministry" the premiership
of Canning.

B

hundred days of Canning ", as it was felicitously
called, was too brief a period for a legislative programme, displaying a scheme of political principles,
to unfold itself. But it was long enough to reveal
that the man himself was an embodied and flesh-
and-blood principle.

II

Canning lingered on the bridge which united or
separated two widely diverse periods—periods as
different in many respects as is the age of Horace
and of Vergil from that of Lord Northcliffe and
Horatio Bottomley. I saw this passage in the
first book of a brilliant young writer the other
day : " It is strange to picture a meeting between Sir Roger de Coverley and Mr. Gradgrind ;
between [Dr.] Johnson . . . and Keats ; but
Wellington and Canning would have met, with
instant recognition and on equal terms, Walpole
and Carteret." [1] Wellington would indeed have
been at home with Sir Roger and all at sea with
Mr. Gradgrind ; but Canning, though himself a
poetic imitator of Pope and of Dryden, was sufficiently modern to admire the poems both of Scott
and of Byron. Similarly he had the dubious
honour of figuring in a slightly disguised form in an
acrimonious debate at the Pickwick Club.[2] But

---

[1] A. A. F. Ramsay, *Idealism and Foreign Policy* (1925), p. 1.

[2] In chapter i. of the *Pickwick Papers*, where Mr. Blotton applied
the term " humbug " to Mr. Pickwick, and qualified it by saying he

he would have been equally at home with Sir Roger
and even more so with Addison ; he could have
exchanged Greek quotations with Carteret and
bandied broad jests with Walpole. For Canning
had a foot in each century. It was said of him,
" On him, as on the St. John of an earlier day, the
air of a gentleman sat with native grace ". And he
certainly much resembled that typically brilliant,
if flashy, representative of the eighteenth century.
Yet Bolingbroke never spoke to crowds as Canning
did, nor would he have had affinities or friendships
with such advanced Whigs as Sir Robert Wilson,
Brougham, or Lord Holland. Still less would
Bolingbroke have been likely to give that most
austere of Benthamites, James Mill, a post in the
India Office, or have been intimate with that most
violent and extreme of all Radical thinkers—William
Godwin.[1] To Wellington—a belated survival from
the eighteenth century—Whigs were detestable,
but Radicals the devil, or devils, in human form.
To Canning they were products, like himself, of a
new age ; men from whom much could be learnt

---

was " a humbug in the Pickwickian sense ". This is a parody of a
scene in the Commons of April 17, 1823, when Canning rose to say that
a statement made by Brougham was false. After much confusion
and the arrival of the sergeant-at-arms Brougham was finally induced
to say that " he was speaking in the parliamentary sense ". The
incident then closed. Hans. *Parl. Debates*, N.S., vol. viii. pp. 1091–1102.

[1] I do not believe the story that Godwin offered Canning the
leadership of the Revolutionary Party in England. But it is a fact
that they were acquainted during the period 1790–3 (J. Macvey Napier's
Select Correspondence, p. 104).

and towards whom something should be conceded. An active programme of reform in the tariff, in the corn laws, in government departments, and a repeal of Catholic grievances, formed a part of the policy of Canning, and thus distinguished him from the reactionary, or Wellingtonian, Tories. He resembled them, and the eighteenth century, in believing the old constitution to be the most exquisite of political combinations, and the reform of the franchise to be the most insidious of steps towards democracy. He hoped never to see the day when the Constitution should be merely " inlaid, for ornament's sake, with a peerage, and topped, by sufferance, with a crown ". All this would have been well understood by Walpole and Carteret, and that fact is not surprising. But it is remarkable that a statesman, so antiquated in some political respects, lived to provide the chief, if not the sole, inspiration of the three foremost among Victorian Prime Ministers. Palmerston had a picture painted of himself with a bust of Canning on a pedestal in the background ; Disraeli "never saw Canning but once ", but he never forgot " the melody of that voice " or " the tumult of that ethereal brow " ; Gladstone, who had literally sat at his feet as a child, declared, " I was bred under the shadow of the great name of Canning ".

III

As though to explain this paradox, Canning's career is divided sharply by the year 1812 into two halves, one working backwards to the past century, the other forwards to the new one. In the first period he struggled vehemently for office and place by means that every eighteenth-century statesman understood ; in the second he displayed powers, and appealed to forces which few of them would have understood, and none of them have dared to use. During the years 1807-9—probably the most critical period of our history—Canning was Foreign Secretary. But for his unfortunate quarrel and duel with Castlereagh just before that time he would certainly have ended the year 1809 as the second man in the Government, and perhaps as the first.

In 1812 Perceval, who had beaten Canning for the premiership, was assassinated, and the political cards were again reshuffled. The Prince Regent (afterwards George IV.) twice commissioned the Marquess Wellesley to form a Government and to co-operate with Canning in the task. No incident attracted more attention in contemporary memoirs, or was less revealed to the public, than these two overtures, which were typical tea-table eighteenth-century intrigues. When they failed Lord Liverpool formed a Government, which though led by the most mediocre of prime ministers, and divided on the most burning of questions, proved the strongest of nineteenth-century Cabinets. It actually lasted for fifteen years.

Even yet Canning's chances were not over. Though there was no possibility of the premiership, Castlereagh, who had become reconciled to him, offered him the office of Foreign Secretary, but declined to surrender to him the lead in the Commons. Had Canning accepted this very handsome offer, he would have been England's Foreign Minister at Vienna in 1815. But he wanted to lead the Commons, and would not, as yet, submit to the lead of Castlereagh. So the ministry was formed without him at the end of 1812. Five years were to elapse before he humbled his pride sufficiently to accept office in this Cabinet, and to submit to the lead of Castlereagh. Ten years were to pass before he succeeded to the leadership in the Commons on Castlereagh's death, and fifteen before he grasped the premiership for a few brief weeks of triumph. Even then he was only fifty-seven.

IV

In the negotiations of the pre-1812 period there was nothing that did not smack of the eighteenth century. There was intrigue in abundance — trafficking with the Regent through chamberlains and goldsticks—trafficking with boroughmongers and with old parliamentary hands. There is never that familiar nineteenth-century feature, a decisive popular or press intervention on behalf of one or other candidate.[1] Yet, though Canning did nothing in these negotiations to suggest novelty, he had already showed originality as Foreign Minister. He published state papers, as every one noted, with unusual frequency, almost in fact as if he wanted the public to know what was going on in diplomacy—which was quite contrary to eighteenth-century ideas. Again, when Spain revolted against Napoleon, Canning said in public that he not only recognised the Spanish nation but that any nation which revolted against Napoleon would at once become England's ally. In those days of respect for constituted authority this bold bid for revolution seemed very startling even when made against Napoleon. It was a foreshadowing of what was to come in the second half of Canning's career, when he, the old Anti-Jacobin, was considered by all diplomats to be the Arch-Revolutionary of Europe.

V

In this very autumn of 1812, Canning severed

[1] The only eighteenth-century exception is perhaps the election of 1784, and even in that it has recently been shown that the old corrupt acts of electioneering and parliamentary management were conspicuous. It is typical that during 1782 and 1783 there were four different ministries and no general election.

himself from eighteenth-century traditions, and
developed a totally new principle. He was asked
to stand for Liverpool. He did so, and headed the
poll in four elections. Liverpool was not what we
should call a popular constituency, though it passed
for such then. It had two members, and about
4000 voters (not far off from the then total number
of all Scotland) of whom Canning's supporters
never exceeded 1650. But these elections had an
extraordinary effect on Canning. They taught him,
first, some contact with the hustings; next, the
needs of a great business community; and last—and
far the most important—they taught him to speak
outside the walls of Parliament, and to appeal to
the people direct. When he entered the Cabinet in
1816, he continued to speak in public; and when
he became Foreign Minister in 1822 and leader of
the Commons, the world continued to hear what it
had never heard before, except at a Mansion House
dinner—a British Minister addressing meetings
beyond the sacred walls of Parliament.

How different was this from the eighteenth-
century Bolingbroke. When refused permission to
speak in the House of Lords, that brilliant orator
never opened his lips again in public. George IV.
thought all this publicity very unseemly, and said
so in private, as did the Duke of Wellington. That
celebrated organ, the *Times*—then somewhat less
urbane than now—told its readers that Mr. Canning

was acting very improperly in rubbing shoulders with business men, and in exciting the clamours of the crowd.

But Canning went on with his speeches, and they led him to victory. All admitted that the Government's success in the elections of 1826 was due to Canning's influence and popularity. There was a highly exciting scene in the Commons on the 12th of December of this year, when Canning announced that he had sent British troops to defend Portugal against Spain, and appealed to public opinion to support him. That support came in a manner which astounded his colleagues, and terrified foreign diplomats. All eyes were at last opened. Canning was suddenly revealed as wielding the thunderbolts of an enormous popularity. The people were on his side ; the press were on his side ; the opposition generally supported him ; in fact his only real opponents were the majority of his reactionary and Tory colleagues in the Cabinet, headed by the Duke of Wellington. And they were swept away on the blast.

VI

Only two months after this Portugal speech, the Prime Minister, Lord Liverpool, was struck with paralysis, and in mid-March, when it was known that he would not again be capable of taking office, a struggle for the vacant premiership began. Canning took an early opportunity of explaining his views to the intriguing Russian Princess Lieven, who delicately insinuated them into the ear of King George IV. They were, at any rate, clear. The Ministry, Canning said, lived by his power and popularity. He governed the press. He was not therefore going to accept any lower post than the premiership, or, at least, he must have, and be known to have, the substantive power of the Premier. George was placed in a difficult position between the imperious Canning and a furious Tory opposition to him, headed by Wellington. After much hesitation, and some mendacity, George yielded, and, on the 10th of April 1827, Canning became Prime Minister, making a coalition between some progressive Tories and the Whigs.

There can be little question that the accession of no man to the premiership ever excited more acclamation outside Parliament. One eye-witness in the vast crowd assembled to see him entering the Commons for the first time as Lord of the Treasury, heard " whispered blessings on many lips ". The editor of the *Examiner* felt it necessary, though he supported the new Premier, to rebuke other journalists for regarding him as the Messiah. For almost a whole month not a single newspaper or pamphlet dared utter a word of dissent. The Tory party-managers—Tadpole and Taper—were aghast ; for their own press organs deserted them, borne along by an irresistible tide of feeling. I know no more remarkable expression of popular excitement, except perhaps Gladstone's Midlothian campaign. It actually had the effect of making the *Times* speak politely of King George.

Canning's accession to power is certainly in one sense remarkable. One Whig statesman, afterwards to be Prime Minister himself, refused to join the Government on the ground that " he regarded the son of an actress as *de facto* incapacitated from being Prime Minister of England ". The viler sort of pamphleteers evidently thought this objection a valid one, for they ultimately published the handbills of the theatrical performances of Canning's mother. It is true that when the premiership was held by the son of an actress, a sort of democracy was enthroned in high places. Canning was, indeed, a new man, and a man of the people ; but new men and men of the people had often been high in the Cabinet before. What was strange was for a new man to have the first place—a man not aided, like the elder and younger Pitts and Foxes, by aristocratic connections and friends, but a man who defied them and told them openly that he would " look such proud combinations in the face ".[1] He

---

[1] The old traditions died hard. Viscount Hambleden, who presided at this lecture, related how his father (W. H. Smith) was criticised in the press for standing against J. S. Mill in 1859. The criticism was on the ground that he was a business-man !

had not relied on or made use of the party machine as such. He had smashed it, and that is not an easy thing to do then or now. " That organisation is now so developed that no individual can fight against it ", writes Lord Rosebery, and he shows that it " crushed him (Randolph Churchill) as easily as a parched pea ".[1] But Canning crushed the machine with the steam-hammer of his popularity. He " stampeded " that part of the press which had been high Tory—and some of it never returned to its old allegiance. And his victory over the forces of Eldonian and Wellingtonian Toryism was permanent. All this was done in a brief three months, for at the end of that time the victor met an adversary more formidable than his old colleagues, and the nation which had hardly finished rejoicing at his triumph was plunged in sorrow at his death.

Six months after Canning's death the Duke of Wellington became Prime Minister, and the prospects of this attempt to reconstruct the old anti-Canningite Toryism is told in one of the most interesting of Disraeli's political sketches, *Sybil*. It was believed that Wellington's Ministry would cease only with his life. There was a good parliamentary majority, and a man possessing immortal fame at the head of it. Yet the Government received shock after shock, and within two years

[1] Lord Rosebery, *Miscellanies* (1921), vol. i. 309, 338.

the national hero resigned office amid popular
commotions so violent as to endanger his life. The
old Toryism was beaten and battered beyond
redemption. When it at length emerged from the
maelstrom it was new and regenerated and was
called Conservativism. What were the causes of
this ? One cause certainly was—to paraphrase
Shakespeare—that " Canning was mighty yet ".
His blow at high Toryism had been deadly ; for it
came from within the ranks. " The rise of Mr.
Canning ", writes Disraeli in the third chapter of
Sybil, " long kept down by the plebeian aristocracy
of Mr. Pitt as an adventurer, had shaken parties to
their centre ". And just at the moment when
party principles were confused, appeared the
influence of a man and of public opinion outside
the walls of Parliament. The man died, but the
secret of his power was revealed, and it was by
using this key that the Whigs unlocked the gates of
office.

The enormous popularity which Canning had
acquired was transferred during his premiership
from the old Tory party to himself, to the Whigs,
and to the new Tories. It enabled Canning to cast
his spell over Palmerston, Disraeli, and Gladstone.
Wellington's premiership simply proved that the
strongest parliamentary majority could not avail
against extreme unpopularity. It showed that the
future lay not with prescription, aristocracy, and

prejudice, but with liberalism, popularity, and enlightenment. These abstract truths were more simply expressed when a new man aspired to the premiership, when the public supported his claim, and the King yielded to his demand. That event showed that the ship of State had pushed off from the safe and solid shores of the eighteenth century, and was navigating the dangerous waters of the nineteenth.

THE DUKE OF WELLINGTON

By Sir CHARLES OMAN

I

WITH all their various faults and weaknesses, the Prime Ministers of the nineteenth century were none of them destitute of capacity of sorts—though party historians have done their best to write down the practical abilities of Addington and Perceval, of Goderich and Aberdeen, and Lord John Russell. But eminence and capacity do not necessarily make a man a good prime minister. And it is curious to find that the greatest historical figure of the first half of the century, the victor of Waterloo, was on the whole the most unlucky adventurer in the paths of supreme governance that our political annals can show. If he had died a few years after the peace of 1815, he might have been called *felix opportunitate mortis*. No historian could have set limits to his possible career as the guardian of the British Empire and its old traditions. But alas! it was a case of *omnium consensu capax imperii, nisi imperasset*—all would have judged him capable of conducting the affairs of the State in the most admirable fashion; but unfortunately the responsibility came to him; he accepted it, not too willingly, and his record was most disappointing. He was a great man, a shrewd man, an honest and straightforward man, but his personal mentality, his political theories, and his conception of the duties of a prime minister, were each of them sufficient to render it certain that he would make a most disastrous experiment, if he tried to work that complicated machine, the British cabinet system, in a time of exceptional storm and stress. To any one who has studied Wellington as a general, and toiled through the vast tomes of his military correspondence, it cannot be denied that a study of the somewhat smaller mass of his political correspondence, during the years that followed Waterloo, brings not only disappointment but surprise. The man was not a mere master of strategy and tactics, but a shrewd observer of everything that came under his eye, a good judge of character, possessed of a keen (if rarely displayed) sense of humour. Casual remarks and table talk show that he had a competent knowledge of history and even of literature. He could appreciate a telling classical quotation, while observing that his own classics were those of an Eton boy in the Remove; and he made occasional Shakespearian allusions. It is impossible to deal with his political aberrations as those of a mere old soldier, wandering about in worlds not realised, and making blunders from want of experience.   It is too often forgotten that he had been in high ministerial office — as Secretary for Ireland—before ever he went out to Portugal in 1808, and had had much experience of politics (especially of their seedier side) while dealing with the place-hunters of Dublin—and of Westminster.   He was not incapable of friendship, and could be kind and considerate when dealing with children, young people (such as schoolboys, aide-de-camps, and, most especially, young charming ladies) and old personal d̠ ⌐ ⌐nts. And yet the record of his politica̠ ⌐ ⌐ one of a series of colossal errors, and the in̠pression which he made on all save a very few of his contemporaries was that of a would-be autocrat, a bleak and frigid formalist, who could occasionally leave a scar that could never be forgotten, by some sardonic word or heartless act.

Perhaps this should have been expected by those who had studied his military career.   There never was a successful general, save perhaps Frederic the Great, who was so little loved and idolised by the troops whom he had led to innumerable victories.   " The sight of his long nose among us, on a battle morning was worth 10,000 men, any day of the week ", wrote one of his veterans.   But though he was feared and respected he was never

C

loved. Or, as a contemporary puts it, " I know
that it has been said that Wellington was not what
may be called popular ; still the troops possessed
great confidence in him ; nor did I ever hear a
single individual express an opinion to the contrary ". The greatest soldier of his age was not
popular with the officers and men of his victorious
army—and why ? Because he did nothing to
earn their love ; he looked upon them as admirable
tools for the task that had been set him, and he
took immense pains to see that those tools were
kept in good order—his assiduous attention to
their food, pay, and clothing contrasted strongly
with Napoleon's haphazard methods. But he was
a hard master, sparing of praise, lavish with censure,
often brusque to the edge of brutality with officers.
Of the rank and file he said words that can never
be pardoned : " They are the scum of the earth—
English soldiers are fellows who have enlisted for
drink—that is the plain fact, they have *all* enlisted
for drink ". For any notion of appealing to the
men's better feelings, or swaying them by sentiment, he expressed supreme contempt. " I have
no idea of any great effect being produced on
British soldiers ", he once said before a Royal Commission, " by anything but the fear of immediate
corporal punishment " ! When Queen Victoria,
then quite a girl, expressed her wish to review her
Guards, he discouraged the proposal—" As to the

soldiers, I know them, they won't care about it one sixpence. It is a childish fancy because she has read about Queen Elizabeth at Tilbury " !

The same thing happened with his political subordinates in after life. Wellington was suspicious, autocratic, sparing of thanks, ruthless in administering snubs and rebukes, possessed of a very long memory for offences, and a very short memory for services. He broke with old political friends (if friends they could be called) in the same callous fashion with which he broke with his own relatives. Every one will remember how he boycotted for nearly twenty years his own brother, Lord Wellesley, the great Viceroy of India, who had given him his first step in the ladder of promotion—the cause of rupture being a purely political difference of opinion. If he had any true friends at all they were either mere personal dependants and satellites, such as Arbuthnot, Croker, or Gurwood, or Gleig, or Alava, or young people of his own entourage to whom he could play the part of Nestor, or of the benevolent uncle of comedy, such as Lord Stanhope. For those who might have been considered his contemporaries and his equals he had never any real tie of affection.

The reason of this was, as a trenchant critic observed, that the Duke had an intellectual contempt for his social equals, and a social contempt for his intellectual equals. This sounds like a hard saying,

but is roughly true. He looked down from the
height of his intellectual superiority on the docile
peers who followed his odd political changes with
puzzled obedience, and grew testy when they
persisted in trying to think for themselves on
occasion. He acknowledged that " party management "—the art of suffering fools gladly—was not
his strong point. In a passing moment of self-
recognition he once observed, " When the Duke of
Newcastle addressed me a letter on the subject of
forming an Administration, I treated him with
contempt. No man *likes* to be treated with contempt. I was wrong." But such moments of
insight came rarely. The Duke was utterly careless of the *amour propre* of his subordinates. Imagine the feelings of a Marquis holding a very high
official position on receiving an important docu-
ment with the endorsement, " This is for your
personal information : I do not want any observation or suggestions on it." Why add the last half-
sentence ? The topic discussed was entirely within
the scope of the Marquis's sphere of duty. Undoubtedly Wellington was justified in believing that
his intellectual powers were superior to those of
most of his subordinates—but there was no reason
to let them see that he thought so.

This was unwise and tactless. Far more unhappy, however, was his ill-concealed consciousness of social superiority towards intellectual equals.

Like Lord Byron he was never able to forget that
he was, what he once spoke of himself as being, a
" sprig of the nobility ".   He had a profound distrust of " new men ", and he looked upon people
like Canning or Huskisson as strange leaders for
the old aristocratic party.   I doubt if he ever
forgot that even Sir Robert Peel was but the son
of a wholesale manufacturer.   Canning was certainly to him an adventurer, of doubtful gentility,
who " showed avowed hostility to the landed
aristocracy of this country ".   Occasionally this
class-feeling flashed out in words which even the
admiring Gleig cannot but call " lacking in deli-
cacy ", as when in the presence of his whole staff
he taunted an unfortunate major of Engineers with
being the son of a duke's butler.   But this distressing story should be read *in extenso* in the narrative
of the worthy Chaplain-General.   A comment on
it is another *obiter dictum*, viz. that he could never
like officers promoted from the ranks, " their fault
always was not being able to resist drink—their
low origin then came out, and you never could
perfectly trust them, and I have *never* known an
officer raised from the ranks turn out well, nor the
system answer ".   This unhappy contempt (I can
use no other word), intellectual and social, for those
with whom he had to work, great and small, would
not have been fatal to Wellington's power as a
statesman if he had been more tactful, or as he

would have called it, more hypocritical. But his honesty hindered : as he once observed he " hated humbug ", and would never flatter, cajole, or conciliate. His honesty was of the form that ran over the edge of brusqueness into occasional brutality. When his devoted adherent Croker wrote to him, in great agony of mind, a four-sided letter setting forth his reasons for resigning his seat in Parliament, after the passing of the Reform Bill, the Duke replied in four lines : " I have received your letter. I am very sorry that you do not intend to be again elected to serve in Parliament. I cannot conceive for what reason." This, when Croker had given him four pages of laboured reasons, could only mean that Wellington regarded these reasons as absurd and unworthy of notice. But even granting this, we must allow that in view of Croker's past services to the cause and the Duke's own person, a few sympathetic words were required. And this omission of the obvious did not come from a dislike to penning long letters. Wellington was the most prolix of correspondents, and would write several pages to advertising doctors who offered him their medicines, or to ladies who sent him trumpery presents. It is true that in inditing such replies he had the opportunity of employing his mordant power of satire. To the doctor he wrote : " As I am attended by the best medical advisers in England, I cannot make use of salves sent me

by a gentleman (however respectable) of whom I
know nothing, and who knows nothing of my case
but what he has read in the newspapers ". The
letter to the officious lady ends with : " The Duke
desires Miss Fiffe to inform him in what manner
her box may be returned to Edinburgh. He gives
notice that if he does not receive an answer by
return of post, the box and its contents will be
thrown into the fire." Wellington, obviously, did
not understand the use of the waste-paper basket,
in dealing with bores and pushing people. He had a
high sense of his own dignity—but this was not the
way to protect it.

II

As to the art of Cabinet government and the
perversity of political colleagues, the Duke has left
a very amusing *obiter dictum*, which may be found
in the diary of Lady Salisbury, for many years one
of the two women with whom he condescended to
talk politics. " One man in the Cabinet wants
one thing, and one another : they agree to what I
may say in the morning, and then in the evening
up they start with some crotchet which deranges
the whole plan. I have not been used to that in
the earlier part of my life. I have been accustomed
to carry on things in quite a different way. I
assembled my officers and laid down my plan, and
it was carried into effect without any more words."

In short, the Duke's conception of the organisation of a Cabinet was that the prime minister should give orders, and the rest should obey them without discussion. It is curious to note that many years before, as far back as 1812, when his brother, Wellesley, threw up his position in Lord Liverpool's Cabinet because his proposals were often over-ruled, Wellington wrote to him in sympathetic terms that " the republic of a Cabinet is but little suited to any man of taste or of large views ". At that same crisis Liverpool had thought well to explain to Wellington what he, as a prime minister, considered to be the working of a Cabinet. " Lord Wellesley says that he has not the weight in the Government that he expected when he accepted office. But government through a Cabinet is necessarily *inter pares*, in which each member must expect to have his opinions and his dispatches canvassed. And their previous friendly canvass of opinions and measures appears necessary, under a constitution where all public acts of ministers will be hostilely debated in Parliament."

It is easy to see why Lord Liverpool held the premiership for fifteen continuous years, and why Wellington smashed up his Cabinet and his party in three. No body of ministers will consent for long to have their policy dictated to them in the form of military orders, criticism of which is regarded as insubordination if not as mutiny. More especially

will this be the case when the Prime Minister
suddenly makes a *volte-face* in policy, and takes up
measures which his colleagues regard as contra-
vening the fundamental creed of their party. Such
was the fate of Sir Robert Peel and of Mr. Gladstone
in later years. But I think that even Mr. Gladstone, who was a man obstinately convinced of the
righteousness of his own most unexpected and
inexplicable mental processes, was less shocked and
less surprised at the conduct of his colleagues than
was Wellington under similar conditions. " What's
the meaning of a party if they don't follow their
leaders ? " he exclaimed to Lord Salisbury. " Damn
'em : let them go." He was not the man who
could talk or think of " educating his party ".
Conscious of his own great ability, still more conscious of the want of ability in the great mass of
his supporters, he thought that they owed him
military obedience—" theirs not to reason why ".
Like Mr. Gilbert's soldier in *Iolanthe*, he felt that
the sight of a group of dull M.P.s in close proximity,
each one trying to think for himself, was enough to
disturb any man's equanimity. His ideal colleague
would have been Sir Joseph Porter, K.C.B., in
another of Mr. Gilbert's immortal works :

> Who always voted at his party's call,
> And never thought of thinking for himself at all.

What an ideal First Lord of the Admiralty for a

Wellington Cabinet! But the Duke might perhaps
have objected to what he would have called the
vulgar origins of a pettifogging attorney.

III

Wellington accepted the position of Prime
Minister, after Canning had been worried to his
grave in 1827, as the avowed leader of the Tory
party. Unfortunately the Tory party was rent by
ill-concealed dissensions between the bulk of its
members, who were still in the state of mentality
caused by the twenty odd years of the great war
with France, and the minority, who thought that
the times of political stagnation should come to an
end, and that improvements of various kinds might
be made in the details, though not in the funda-
mentals of the Constitution. To both sections
Wellington was at first the *deus ex machina* whose
ripe wisdom and tried ability would guide the State
out of the difficulties which had been obvious for so
many recent years. To people like Lord Eldon, or
Lord Sidmouth, to the majority of the House of
Lords, the Duke appeared destined to vindicate the
old Tory creed with all the prestige of his dominating personality and his unrivalled reputation. I
suppose that it was, in effect, inevitable that he
should offend one or other of these sections : to
have kept both Canningites and admirers of Lord

Eldon and the Duke of Cumberland in his Cabinet would have required talents of management surpassing even those of Lord Liverpool. The misfortune of Wellington was that he continued to irritate both factions, and to be accused by each of inconsistency, and perverse illogical autocracy. When he passed his Catholic Relief Bill, the old Protestant Church-and-State party regarded him as a traitor to the Altar and the Crown. When he definitely rejected all proposals for Parliamentary Reform, and directed the House of Lords to throw out Lord Grey's first Reform Bill in October 1831, the Tories who believed in the necessity of some sort of a change in the national representation, the " waverers " as he called them, naturally concluded that he was what we should now call a " die-hard ", or a " last ditcher ". And yet in May 1832 he was found endeavouring to patch up a Cabinet which would engage to pass a Reform Bill of his own, guaranteed to be liberal rather than " moderate "— though six months before he had declared in very solemn phrases that the present state of the constitution of the House of Commons was ideal, and that it could not be improved or rendered more satisfactory than it was in 1831. To the old Tories his dealings with the Catholic Relief Bill looked like cynical opportunism. Not only to old Tories, but to Canningites also, his proposal to pass a Reform Bill in 1832 appeared not only inappropriate

but immoral. Sir Robert Peel put on paper the
statement that he considered that to take any part
in producing such a Bill would be a personal
degradation to himself—it would be to assume
responsibility for changes which he had declared
a hundred times over to be dangerous and
revolutionary.

Yet Wellington was undoubtedly neither an
opportunist, ready to change his policy in any way
that would keep him in office, nor a deliberate
hypocrite, nor a man destitute of any real political
creed. He was simply one who honestly believed
that he and his personality were the only things
that stood between Great Britain and anarchical
revolution. Not that he thought that Lord Grey
or Lord Melbourne, or even Lord Brougham, were
themselves Jacobins, or deliberately resolved to
ruin their country, but that he was under the
impression that they were recklessly opening the
flood-gates through which the inundation must
come, to sweep them and all Whigs as well as all
Tories to destruction. Hence it was his duty to
keep them out of office, even if it had to be done by
fighting a series of rear-guard actions, by defending
each outlying position, and retiring to the next
when his flank was turned or his centre driven in.
The Acts which imposed disabilities on Catholics
were an untenable outwork, as he concluded. If
it were no longer possible to maintain it, he had

better evacuate it himself, rather than endure a
ruinous defeat in defending it. The constitution
of the unreformed Parliament was a much more
important item in his system of fortification against
Jacobinism ; but if it had to be sacrificed, it was
better that the details of the retreat should be
settled by himself, rather than by the enemy.

IV

The underlying idea which lay at the base of all
Wellington's conceptions as to the state of the
realm during the years of his political activity, was
that revolution was possible—very possible—in
England, if things were suffered to drift, and mere
Whig parliamentarians, working for their party
ends, were allowed to get hold of the helm of the
State. Looking back at the troubles of 1820-37
across the long and tranquil reign of Queen Victoria,
we find it hard to realise the mental outlook of
many intelligent people, who believed in all honesty
that " red ruin and the breaking up of laws " were
at hand, and that any and every means—from the
use of the bayonet to the abandonment of one's own
cherished political views—might have to be used
to avert impending chaos. But let us remember
some of our own misgivings during the General
Strike of May 1926. To regard the Tories of
the post-war period 1815-32 as besotted alarmists

is to do them wrong. There was much to justify their view of the state of affairs : they recalled, as a memory of their early youth, the state of London during the Gordon Riots. When they were grown men they had seen the Irish Rebellion of 1798, the mutinies of the Nore and Spithead, and the murderous if futile plot of Colonel Despard, the first revolutionary who invented the notion of a " soviet of soldiers and workmen"—for this was precisely Despard's scheme of organisation. Though Great Britain had experienced no revolution in the French style, she had seen intermittent riot, sedition, and outrage, all through the first twenty years of the nineteenth century. In the lean days after Waterloo things had been worse than ever— as witness Peterloo and the Six Acts. I imagine that, though he seldom talked about it, the Duke had not forgotten that he had been within a measurable distance of assassination, when Arthur Thistlewood's desperadoes planned their raid upon the Cabinet dinner at Lord Harrowby's house in Grosvenor Square. If one takes the trouble to wade through lists of forgotten incidents, whose record is preserved only in Annual Registers or contemporary political pamphlets, one ceases to regard the views of Wellington and Peel, or even those of Lord Eldon and Lord Sidmouth, with the pitying contempt bestowed upon them by the Liberal historians of the next generation.

Wellington, it must be confessed, had this obsession in the strongest form. In one curious letter he wrote that he had spent the better part of his life not merely in war, but in civil war. He was under the impression that the passing of the Reform Bill would lead to " revolution ", with massacres like those of Paris in 1792–3 thrown in. Even after the Bill had been passed, and the new Parliament was sitting, he expressed his views that the first stage of the movement was over, but that democracy in its worst form having been introduced, the destruction of the monarchy and the Constitution could not be long delayed. " The change in the position of the country may be gradual, it may be effected without civil war, and may occasion as little sudden destruction of private property as possible—but future changes will go on *ad nauseam* —a shame and disgrace to the public men of this day." This was written as late as 1835. He sometimes envisaged the possible details of the English revolution, and allowed that if it became sufficiently wild and dangerous, he might be driven to take up the position of a military dictator. At least this is the only rational meaning that I can attach to one observation to the effect that if the worse came to the worst the man should not be wanting. " My opinion is that a democracy once set going must sooner or later work itself out in anarchy ", he said, " and that some sort of despotism must then come

to restore society ". From the very drastic and
complete military arrangements which he made
when preparing to face the Chartists, on the day of
their proposed march on Westminster, I do not
doubt that if Wellington had been in office, as
Prime Minister or Commander-in-Chief, and faced
by an open outbreak of organised insurrection, he
would have suppressed it most effectively, with or
without much bloodshed. But if he were not in
office his scrupulous regard for legality would have
made it almost certain that he would not resort to
force, except in the single case of an actual attack
on the Crown—in such case his loyalty would have
over-ruled his legality. In the crisis of 1831–32
some Tories proposed to found " counter-associa-
tions ", " constitutional leagues "—practically what
we should now call clubs of " Fascisti ". Even
Sir Robert Peel dallied with the idea—" if the
supporters of the Government are allowed to
organise armed clubs for the purpose of attack—
the only safety is in preparation for defence. I
certainly, if necessity arises, shall form, and counsel
others to form, quiet unostentatious associations for
the purpose of self-defence against unprovoked
aggression ". The Duke pondered the matter and
finally refused to authorise the foundation of such
societies : his point of view was that there was
a Government in power responsible to the King : to
use force, or threats of force, against such a Govern-

ment, so long as it was legally constituted, was not
permissible to the party which called itself the
representative of order and legality. Yet Wellington believed that Lord Grey was letting loose the
" red spectre " ; that whatever the Whigs might
intend, they would be swept away by forces which
they could not control, and that " the Revolution
would devour its own children ", as in the France
of the Girondins and the Jacobins. But only when
the King and the Two Houses should be attacked by
open violence would it be permissible for private
persons to intervene in arms.

V

It must be confessed that the Duke went very
near to provoking the crisis which he dreaded, when
in May 1832, after the rejection of the Reform Bill
by the House of Lords, he prepared to take office
once more as the head of a Tory administration.
Fortunately his chosen colleagues would not back
him, and the scheme came to nought. But if he
had actually assumed the reins of power, as the
King's minister, it is pretty certain that widespread
disorder, to which the Bristol Riots would have been
a trifle, would have broken out all over the realm.
And if such outbreaks had occurred, it is equally
certain that Wellington would have thought it his
duty to use armed force against them in a ruthless

D

and effective fashion. He would have deplored the
necessity, but it would have been his duty to protect
the Crown and the Constitution. That on assuming
office he intended to bring forward a Reform Bill
of his own would have gone for nothing. His
public condemnation of any sort of change in the
House of Commons had been so violent and so
frequent that it would have been considered a
piece of cynical hypocrisy if he had professed his
intention to bring in a " moderate " or a " liberal "
Reform Bill of his own. His resumption of
office would have been ascribed to mere love of
power and place ; his Bill would inevitably have
been called a solemn sham. Sir Robert Peel was
wiser than his chief, when he refused to touch the
scheme, declaring that to pass Reform Bills was
the proper business of the Whigs, and that it would
amount to political immorality for Tories to bring
in legislation which they regarded as dangerous
and destructive. This Wellington could not, or
would not, see. His odd reply was that he should
be ashamed to show his face in the streets if he had
failed to do his best to serve the King in a moment
of emergency. The humour of the situation was
that the King was at the moment anything but
anxious to be served in this particular way, though
he had been forced to apply to Wellington when
Lord Grey tendered his resignation.

Wellington's formal justification for his curious

policy was that he was, as he phrased it, "the retained servant of the Sovereign of this Empire", the sworn and salaried employé of the Crown. As a loyal subordinate it was his duty to do his best for his employer, according to his lights, however distasteful and even humiliating such service might be. "The King's Government must be carried on *somehow*" was another of his dicta, and believing as he did that the advent of the Whig party to office would lead to general ruin in the near future, it was his duty to keep them out of power, or to check (so far as he could) their attempts to hack away what he considered essential parts of the Constitution. All his duty was to the Crown— even when the Crown was worn by George IV.

VI

But the personality of the Sovereign under whom the first two years of his ministry were spent was one of his greatest difficulties. There can seldom have been two men whose mentalities were more offensive to each other than George IV. and Wellington. The King was selfish, thriftless, idle, ostentatious, pleasure-loving, capable of any trick or evasion; yet extremely clever withal, an actor of talent, full of amusing conversation, capable when he chose of managing a negotiation as well as the most unscrupulous diplomatist, a fascinating

host, if a most unreliable friend. He spent his life
in finding plausible excuses for shirking unpleasant
duties, but discharged pleasant ones with brilliant
success and undeniable tact. The Duke was unostentatious, even ascetic ; he had a perfect genius
for bleak discomfort in the conduct of his private
life. He was obsessed, even beyond the bounds of
wisdom, by the desire to carry out every formal
duty in the most complete fashion. The amount
of prolix and often unnecessary private letters
which he wrote causes wonder ; he got up every
morning at five o'clock to deal with them. The
King was seldom dressed by noon, but when he
did dress it was a triumph. Wellington hated full-
dress uniform—he fought the whole Peninsular War
in a grey frock-coat and a plumeless cocked hat,
and only brought out his decorations—he had an
inconvenient bushel of them—for very great occasions. The King was a gourmet : the Duke did
not care what he ate. In 1814 he once dined at
Paris with the Arch-Chancellor Cambacérès, the
greatest epicure of France. Cambacérès watched
the Duke working through his dinner with obvious
want of appreciation of its excellence. At last he
called his attention to a dish on which special
talent had been employed—was it not attractive ?
" Oh yes ", replied Wellington, " quite good—but
I never notice what I eat ". " *Mon Dieu*," exclaimed the ex-Chancellor, " and you come here to

dine with *me* ! " In his old age the Duke was so
neglectful of his meals that he sometimes fell in a
fainting fit from having forgotten how long it was
since he last tasted food. When he got into official
converse with his Sovereign, the difficulty was to
keep King George to the point—if the point was
one on which he did not want to be pressed. He
was a lively conversationalist, and adroit at getting
away from distasteful topics. Wellington, as he
said himself, had " no small talk ", and had to be
harking back to the question of the moment in
spite of the discursiveness of a master whose
frivolity was a terrible trial to him. It is on record
that on his first appearance as prime minister the
King did everything that could revolt his stiff and
formal servant. George was found in bed, in a
dirty silk dressing-gown and a turban night-cap,
but in high good humour. " Arthur ", he chuckled,
" the late Cabinet is defunct ", and then proceeded
to give a ludicrous dramatic rendering of the behaviour of the various members of the Goderich
administration, at their final interview with him to
give up their seals of office, mimicking the peculi-
arities of each with much accuracy and animation.
Wellington did not like mumming, and he did not
like dirty dressing-gowns. I do not think that he
liked being called " Arthur," and he regarded this
moment as the most serious in his life, when he
was called to an arduous situation, and what he

considered a very disagreeable duty. His feelings
may be easily imagined.

Loyalty to the Crown turned out to be a very
odd business, when the Crown was worn by George
IV. It often consisted in what His Majesty called
" bullying ", *i.e.* in compelling him by steady and
constant pressure to do things which he did not like.
Considering the thorough knowledge of the King's
mentality which he possessed, the Duke was particularly irritated when his master took up the line
of resistance called " conscientious objection ".
This was employed all through the time of the
Catholic Relief Bill. The King kept impressing on
the Duke that he was afraid that his coronation
oath and his religious scruples forebade him to
give his royal assent to the Act. This method had
been tried by George III. on William Pitt with
complete success : every one *did* know that the
elder king possessed a conscience, and a very
obstinate one. But the exhibition of an active
Protestant conscience by George IV. was not a
convincing move. " I make it a rule ", said Wellington, " never to interrupt him, and when he
turns the conversation and tries to get rid of the
subject, I let him talk himself out, and then
quietly put before him again the matter in question, so that he cannot escape from it ! " On
February 1, 1829, George IV. signed the draft of
the King's Speech which committed him to Catholic

Relief: on March 3 he suddenly revived his scruples and protested that he had been misled and deceived. The ministers offered to resign—nay did so, after a very distressing and emotional interview. The Cabinet thought that all was over : but Wellington had made out that His Majesty was only bluffing. "Don't be afraid", he said ; "before to-morrow morning, depend upon it, I shall hear from the King again". And so it was, the bluff having been called. Before he got to bed that night Wellington received a five-line note from Windsor. "God knows what pain it costs me to write these words : under the circumstances you have my consent to proceed with the measure." And this was what the Duke called serving the Crown.

VII

It must be confessed that if the King's political views, or alleged views, were sometimes surprising, the Duke's expressed opinions occasionally seem astounding to us, looking back as we do over the long Victorian régime that intervenes between our day and his. Some of the things which he defended were indefensible—he spoke out fearlessly on behalf of Rotten Boroughs. "I confess that I see in the members for the 30 Rotten Boroughs men who would preserve the state of property as it is, who would maintain by their votes the Church of

England, the Union with Scotland and Ireland, our
colonies and possessions, our national honour. I
think that it is the presence in Parliament of this
sort of man, with the county gentlemen and bankers
and great manufacturers, that makes the House
of Commons differ from a Foreign Chamber of
Deputies. It is by means of the representation of
those close boroughs that the great proprietors
of England participate in political power. We
can't spare these men, or exchange them for members elected by great towns under an extended
franchise." Wellington once issued the gnome
that *all* reform is bad and dangerous, because all
reform ends by being Radical. He defended the
Purchase System in the Army ; the lavish use of
corporal punishment. He disliked education,
opposing at once staff colleges and army school-
masters. He sometimes spoke of the good of the
" landed interest ", where we should speak of
the good of the State. All this, I think, came
directly or indirectly from the guiding theory
which we spoke of before, the notion that the
English Revolution was at hand, and that if he
could not stop it, he could at any rate oppose
anything that pushed it into the less-immediate
future.

That this was a melancholy outlook, and a de-
pressing scheme of life, I think that Wellington
himself would have agreed. The fear of revolution

never left him, and in his extreme old age he
thought, during the Chartist troubles of 1848, that
it was once more growing imminent, and turned
all that remained of his faculties to the task of
devising a method for dealing with civil war in the
streets of London. His plan was excellent, and
would no doubt have been effective ; but it was
never tested. Indeed we can see now that the
danger was not what the men of that day expected
it to be.

It is some consolation to the admirers of
Wellington that he at least enjoyed a sort of
Indian summer in his declining years : he lived
to see his fears of immediate chaos, so acute in
1832, die away. He survived to see Conservative
ministers in power, and a popular sovereign on the
throne which in 1830 had seemed to totter. What
probably affected less his Spartan set of mind was
that he survived to find himself no longer the much-
hated representative of Reaction and the enemy of
the mob. He himself never forgot the broken
windows of Apsley House : but the rest of the
world did ; and he figured in the memory of the
generation that had grown up since Reform Bill
times as a sort of historical monument, absolutely
straight and true to type. He knew what was
expected of him : " I am the Duke of Wellington,
and must do as the Duke of Wellington doth ", was
one of his touches of sardonic humour. But it

was also one more indication of the fact that he
regarded an inflexible adherence to his own peculiar
code of duty as the highest obligation.

> But above all, to thine own self be true,
> Thou canst not then be false to any man.

SIR ROBERT PEEL

By Sir RICHARD LODGE

" His life was one of perpetual education."—DISRAELI.

I

IN an often quoted phrase, which may serve as my text, Adam Smith speaks of " that crafty and insidious animal vulgarly called a statesman or politician ". [1] In the eighteenth century these last terms may have had an identical meaning. But since then there has been a growing tendency to differentiate them. A politician is still, as always, a man who plays an active and it may be a prominent part in political life. And in modern times it means a party politician. The political history of England for two centuries has been the history of parties. Since the reign of Anne administrations have been labelled by party names—Whig or Tory, Liberal or Conservative, and in recent times Unionist and Labour. The sequence is occasionally interrupted by coalitions, but we have been told on high authority that England does not love

[1] *Wealth of Nations*, book iv. chap. ii. (ed. Nicholson), p. 190.

43

coalitions, and their rarity seems to justify the assertion. And even coalitions imply the existence of parties to form them. The first act of a would-be politician is to join a party. And the qualities which raise a man to prominence in a party are very much the same as those which were conspicuous in the time of Adam Smith. A politician may still be described, without any undue depreciation, as an " insidious and crafty animal ".

But statesmanship has come to imply something more than political activity or even than political pre-eminence. There are many politicians : there are few statesmen. A statesman, I take it, is a man who performs some constructive work, who guides a country through a difficult crisis, who restores its prosperity and self-confidence after a period of disaster or distress, whose career marks an epoch in its history. A few concrete instances, taken from our own history, may serve to illustrate and enforce my interpretation. Statesmanship may be attributed to Oliver Cromwell, who maintained order and discipline when the constitutional and administrative machinery had been broken to pieces ; to Clarendon, who rebuilt the constitution after the turmoil of civil war and after the anarchy that followed Cromwell's death, and built it on foundations so durable that they have not yet been destroyed ; to the elder Pitt, who raised the nation from the slough of despond to which it had been reduced by those eminent politicians, the brothers Pelham; to the younger Pitt, whose career is associated with the revival of England after the war of the American revolt and with the guidance of the country through the storms that arose from and after the French Revolution.

These men, however, were hardly, except possibly the last, politicians in Adam Smith's sense. Oliver Cromwell, great man as he was, could not impose a republican constitution on a country which did not want it, and only maintained his rule by the support of an invincible army. Clarendon, invaluable as were his services, was not crafty enough to retain the favour of the King and the gentry, whom he had restored to power, and fell a victim to the intrigues of men who were his inferiors in everything but political craft. The elder Pitt had a political career which is not wholly to his credit, but, when he rose to power, he disdained party, left political management to the practised hands of Newcastle, and devoted himself to the task of saving the country. When he fell from office, he was unquestionably the greatest of living Englishmen, but his lack of party support condemned him to political impotence. His son owed his prolonged tenure of office, not so much to his political skill, in which he was not deficient, but partly to the gross faults of his predecessors, and partly to the circumstances of the time, which obscured previous party divisions and made opposition to the Government appear to be synonymous with treachery to the national cause. I doubt whether Adam Smith would have called any of these men, and certainly not the first three, insidious and crafty animals.

Since the death of Pitt the race of statesmen who were comparatively free from party obligations has largely died out. It is the characteristic —some might say the curse—of that system of party government which Great Britain has given to the world, that a man can hardly rise to political eminence without having served an apprenticeship, and generally a long apprenticeship, in party politics. In other words, he must be an insidious and crafty animal before he can become something greater and better. He may have all the qualities of a great statesman, but he has little chance of showing them unless he also has the support which the party machine alone can give him, and which he must earn by party service. It is true that the necessary apprenticeship need no longer be served in the House of Commons. It may be done in municipal and local politics, as by Joseph Chamberlain, or in political journalism, as by John Morley, or in political agitation, as by Cobden and Bright, or in more modern times by activity as a leader in trade disputes. But, whatever the theatre, the nature of the service is the same, and its object is to procure party recognition and prominence.

There are two sets of men to whom the general rule does not apply. One of these includes the members of the permanent Civil Service—condemned by the traditions of their profession to stand aloof from party, the men whose firm grasp of the administrative machine is concealed by the prominence of the short-lived parliamentary mouthpieces who represent or misrepresent them. There may be great statesmen or potential statesmen among them, but we do not know it because their activity is hidden and unadvertised, and when they retire with a pension, and it may be in recent times with a peerage, it is too late for them to offer the necessary sacrifice to the idol of party. What we lose by this burial of first-class ability is as difficult to estimate as is the greatness of the service which they render from behind the veil. The other class consists of the eminent men who serve the country at a distance, either as diplomatists in foreign courts, or as pro-consuls in outlying parts of the Commonwealth. Such men, as for instance Lord Dufferin and Lord Cromer, may have the hall-marks of statesmanship, but in the nature of things it cannot be displayed in the central political arena. Some who have served in these outposts, like Macaulay and Lord Curzon, have returned early enough to resume a political position which they had only vacated for a while ; but it may be questioned whether their temporary banishment, while it added to their experience and their usefulness, did not handicap them in the race with contemporaries who never relaxed their hold upon the mechanism of party strife. The only man in my own generation who rose to eminence at home irrespective of party, the late Lord Milner, owed his exceptional recognition to the abnormal circumstances of the War, and, when these ended, was compelled to return to the obscurity to which his previous career seemed at one time to have permanently condemned him.

I do not propose to discuss the merits or the ethics of party government, though there are signs both in Europe and in the United States that its ascendancy is destined to be seriously threatened. But this prefatory insistence upon the essential connection in the nineteenth century between political eminence and party allegiance is a necessary introduction to any survey of the career of Sir Robert Peel. It is this connection which has given rise to the curious but widespread conviction that the primary virtue of a statesman is consistency ; that desertion of a party is of the nature of disloyalty ; that the transfer from one party to another is *prima facie* evidence of dishonesty ; and that the disruption or destruction of so valuable a bequest from the past as an organised political party is a crime for which no punishment can be too great. It is this which has filled the pages of Hansard with the record of those futile efforts, repeated generation after generation, to answer a speaker's arguments, not by counter-argument, but by producing evidence that he once said something different.

A kindred problem which touches that of consistency is that of the age at which a political career should begin. When a man serves an apprenticeship outside the House of Commons, it may be expected that he enters that assembly with formed and reasoned convictions. But Peel, like Pitt and Gladstone, came to Parliament immediately after graduation at the university. There can be no doubt that all three owed much of their success to the instinctive grip of political conditions and especially of the House of Commons which they gained by their early entry. And it is probable that it can only be acquired with difficulty in any other way. But it is equally clear that in such cases the insistence upon consistency of opinion or even of unbroken party allegiance becomes preposterous. Nobody with the slightest pretensions to ability or to honesty can pledge his future convictions or his future conduct at the age of twenty-one or twenty-two. If he did so, he would be fatally fettered, and his usefulness maimed or destroyed.

II

The chronological sequence of Peel's career is probably familiar to you, but it is necessary to recapitulate its main events. He was born in 1788 on the eve of the French Revolution, and he had grown to manhood before Europe had recovered peace and stability after the turmoil and warfare of which that revolution had been the starting-point. He was descended from a north of England family which had gained wealth in the cotton industry. His father was an active Tory politician, and a devout follower of Pitt, who rewarded his loyalty with a baronetcy in 1800. It is not un-important to remember that the father lived till 1830, and sat in the House of Commons with his distinguished son for twenty years.

In 1801 Peel went to Harrow, where he was the contemporary of Lord Byron, and also of three boys who were destined, like Peel himself, to hold the office of Prime Minister.[1] It may be doubted whether any other school could boast of such distinction in a single generation.

In 1805 Peel matriculated at Christ Church, the most aristocratic college in a university whose intellectual calm had just been broken by the

[1] These were Lord Ripon, Lord Aberdeen, and Lord Palmerston. It may be added that Perceval in the previous generation was also a Harrovian.

institution of the first two honours schools in
classics and mathematics. Three years later he
took his degree with first-class honours in both
schools. He was the first to gain this distinction,
and the reported brilliance of his oral examination
made some sensation in the university and in those
circles in London which were in touch with Oxford.

In the next year, 1809, Peel entered the House
of Commons, an Irish seat being simply bought for
him by his father as a reward for his academic
triumph. Rarely has a raw recruit been more
warmly welcomed by a party in possession of office.
Within twelve months he was appointed Under-
Secretary for the Colonies and War, and as his chief,
Lord Liverpool, was in the Upper House, he was
called upon to explain and defend military opera-
tions in the Peninsula. When on the death of
Perceval, Lord Liverpool became Prime Minister,
he recognised the merits of his youthful subordinate
by promoting him to be Chief Secretary for Ireland.
For six years " Orange " Peel, as he was called by
the opponents of Protestant domination, broke
his teeth on the problem of maintaining order in a
country where the majority of the people considered
lawlessness to be both a patriotic and a religious
duty.

There are three noteworthy episodes in Peel's
Irish administration. One was the formation of
the police force—the original " Peelers " and

" Bobbies ", before the names were transplanted
from Dublin to London—which developed into
the famous Royal Irish Constabulary. Another
was the abortive duel with O'Connell, when Peel
smuggled himself to Ostend, where he waited in
vain for an antagonist who was conveniently
arrested in London. The third was the delivery of
an impressive speech against the Catholic claims in
the House of Commons in 1817 which earned for
him an uncontested return for the University of
Oxford. This was a sudden exaltation from the
pocket boroughs of Cashel and Chippenham, which
had hitherto provided him with a seat, and was a
source of intense gratification both to Peel himself
and to his exultant father.

Peel was sickened by the squalid corruption of
Irish administration, which bulks so largely in his
correspondence during the six years of his chief-
secretaryship, and he was glad to retire from an
uncongenial office in 1818. He had by this time
established his reputation in the House of Commons,
and his admiring contemporaries were convinced
that party leadership must before long fall to his
lot. But for three years he seemed content with
his unfamiliar freedom, and refused more than one
invitation from Lord Liverpool to enter the Tory
Cabinet. It was during this interval that he
married, and thus began the happy family life
which has been disclosed to the world in the

attractive volume of letters edited six years ago by his grandson, the Hon. George Peel. But before his marriage he had rendered one of his greatest services to the country. In 1819 a Bullion Committee, containing Canning, Tierney, and other eminent men, was appointed, and the young Peel, just thirty-one years old, was chosen to be its chairman. In that capacity he drafted the report which led to the Act—generally known as " Peel's Act "—for the resumption of cash payments. This put an end to the depreciation of the currency, and, combined with the later Bank Act of 1844, also due to Peel, gave to Victorian England the priceless boon of a sound monetary system. The part which Peel played is not only creditable in itself, but it also marks a notable advance in independence, as his father, upon whom he was absolutely dependent for his income, was a convinced supporter of inconvertible paper. It was also the first of Peel's inevitable recantations. In 1811, when he knew nothing of political economy, he had voted against the adoption of the same measure when it was recommended by Francis Horner's committee. Eight years later, when he had been compelled to master the subject, he justified his altered attitude, not on the quite tenable ground that circumstances had altered, but by a frank admission that his earlier vote was given in ignorance and in error.

Peel's abstention from office during the three

years 1818–21 saved him from any complicity
in the squalid episode of the Queen's trial, which
led to Canning's temporary retirement from the
ministry. But the Queen's death removed this
difficulty, and at the end of 1821 Peel entered the
Cabinet as Home Secretary in succession to Lord
Sidmouth. A few months later the suicide of
Castlereagh vacated the leadership of the House
of Commons, just as Canning was on the verge of
starting for India as Governor-General. If George
IV. could have had his way, Canning would have
gone to India, and Peel, in spite of his youth and
comparative inexperience, would have become
leader in the Commons with a practically assured
succession to the premiership. But, after a few
weeks of uncertainty, Liverpool insisted upon secur-
ing the services of the more practised lieutenant,
and Canning entered upon his memorable tenure
of the Foreign Office, with the lead in the Lower
House. Peel had no possible ground of complaint,
and for the next four years proved himself a
punctiliously loyal colleague, supporting both the
foreign policy of Canning and the fiscal reforms of
Huskisson. In the administration of his own office
he was eminently successful, in spite of increasing
difficulties in Ireland, and Canning emphatically
declared that he was the best Home Secretary the
country had ever had. His most notable achievement in this period was the reform of the criminal

law, by which he put into practical shape the principal measures which had been so long advocated by Romilly and Mackintosh.

In 1827 Liverpool's long tenure of office was ended by a paralytic stroke. A very difficult situation ensued. From the outset his ministry had been divided on the question of Catholic relief, which had been the predominant domestic problem ever since the Irish Union. George IV., both as Regent and as King, had obstinately adhered to his father's opinion that he could not sanction concessions to the Roman Catholics without a breach of his coronation oath. In deference to this view Liverpool had accepted office with a pledge that Catholic relief should never be brought forward as a Cabinet measure. On the other hand, the question was to be an open one, and individual ministers were to be free to take their own action upon it. This compact, anomalous as it may appear in the present day, had been scrupulously observed. Liverpool himself, sometimes rather half-heartedly, and Wellington and Peel, with more resolution, had opposed the Roman Catholic claims. On the other hand, they had been vehemently advocated by Canning and his supporters, as they had previously been by Castlereagh. This question was the great stumbling-block in 1827. It was clear that the elevation of Canning, whose claims to the premiership on other grounds were incontestable, would alter the balance very decisively in favour of the pro-Catholic party, and on this ground Peel refused to concur in his appointment. It must be remembered that Peel had reason to be specially sensitive on this point. Not only was Ireland within the purview of the Home Department, but also he had formed strong views during his residence in Ireland, and in recent years he had been forced to take a very decided attitude by the fact that he had been the only Protestant minister in the House of Commons. When, in spite of his opposition, a relief Bill had gained a majority in the Commons in 1825, he had offered his resignation, and had only been induced to remain in office by the Prime Minister's urgent remonstrance that his retirement would destroy the ministry,[1] and by the rejection of the Bill in the House of Lords.

Peel's opposition to Canning's premiership was therefore inevitable and openly avowed. And it was recognised by Canning himself as reasonable. On the other hand Canning urged, equally reasonably, that it would be unfair to proscribe the supporters of one side on an admittedly open question. And it was not easy to find a satisfactory rival candidate. Wellington, whom Peel would have wished for, was ruled out at this time, and (rather curiously in view of the immediate future) admitted that he was ruled out, on the ground that it was

[1] See Parker, *Sir Robert Peel*, i. p. 374.

unconstitutional to combine in one hand the highest
civil and military offices. This left Peel himself as
the most eminent of the anti-Catholic Tories, but
it would be an intolerable insult to Canning, after
the decision of 1822, to ask him to serve under his
junior colleague. As a last resource Peel suggested
the selection of some peer as a figure-head, such as
the second Lord Melville, under whom both could
continue to co-operate. But Canning would not
consent to this, and he finally triumphed, not only
on account of his superior claims, but also because
George IV. was induced to believe that Wellington
and the Tory peers were in league, as the Whigs
were said to have been in the early years of George
III., to coerce the King and to deprive him of the
prerogative of selecting his own chief minister.[1]
Canning's appointment was followed by the resignation of Peel, Wellington, Eldon, and the other
opponents of Catholic relief, though it was strenuously denied that their resignation was a concerted act. Wellington not only retired from the
Cabinet but also gave up his military command.
His action was bitterly resented by Canning,
whereas he admitted that Peel's conduct had been
scrupulously straightforward and correct.

Whether concerted or not, the desertion of the
more orthodox Tories compelled Canning to appeal
to a section of the Whigs, and to form a coalition

[1] See Stapleton, *Life of Canning*, iii. p. 314.

ministry by the admission of Lansdown and Tierney. The result was that when Parliament met, Peel found himself for the first time in the position of a leader of opposition. Another result was that he was forced into a virtual alliance with Wellington, with whom his previous relations had been friendly, but by no means intimate. The session was a short one, and Peel was spared from taking a very active part in controversy, as the most acrimonious criticism of the ministry came from Lord Grey and the main body of the Whigs. The subsequent charge by Lord George Bentinck that Peel harried his former colleague into his grave is wholly devoid of foundation. Canning's health had never recovered from a chill contracted at the Duke of York's funeral, and soon after the close of the session he retired to Chiswick to die. George IV., still chafing against the supposed dictation of "King Arthur", as the Duke of Cumberland mischievously called Wellington, refused to return to the Tory leaders, and entrusted Goderich, whom Canning had promoted to lead the House of Lords, with the task of continuing the existing ministry. But between the King, who wished to dictate the choice of a new Chancellor of the Exchequer, and the Whigs, who objected to such royal interference in the filling of particular offices, Goderich found it impossible to manage his Cabinet, much less to govern a kingdom or an empire. And so—as a

" transient and embarrassed phantom "—he wept himself out of office without ever having ventured on a parliamentary session.

Canning's coalition had obviously broken down, and it was in the nature of things a hopeless experiment. Catholic emancipation, the one question on which they were agreed, they were precluded from proposing by the terms on which Canning accepted his appointment from the Crown. Parliamentary reform, the other great article in the Whig creed, was barred by the resolute opposition of the Prime Minister. Canning, if he had lived, might have fallen less ignominiously than Goderich, but he could not have averted a fall. The King had no longer any alternative, and promptly called in Wellington, who had partially appeased him by resuming the command of the army after Canning's death, in response to an urgent appeal from both the King and Goderich. In spite of his recent admission of disqualification, the Duke did not hesitate to accept the invitation to form a ministry, and his first act was to invite the co-operation of Peel. Peel, who offered no objection to a military prime minister, elected to return to his old office. The selection of colleagues was their joint work and was carried through without regard to the suggestions and objections of the King. Peel's great object was to restore the ministry of Liverpool with its two wings of pro- and anti-Catholics

on the same terms as before. He was so far successful that Huskisson, Palmerston, and the other
soi-disant Tory colleagues of Canning accepted
places in the new Cabinet. But the sores of 1827
were not yet healed, and Huskisson's retirement
on the East Retford Bill, promptly accepted by
Wellington, was followed by the resignation of all
the Canningites. Thus in May 1828 Peel found
himself left in that purely Protestant and in a
sense ultra-Tory ministry whose formation he had
hitherto consistently opposed. It was this truncated and essentially weak administration which
in its first session surrendered to the opposition
on the repeal of the Test and Corporation Acts,
and in the same year was confronted by the problem of the Clare election. It might have been
foreseen. In the General Election of 1826 the
peasant tenants, enfranchised by the Irish Act of
1793, had for the first time followed the priests in
a revolt against their landlords and returned Protestant members pledged to vote for Catholic relief.
Since then their hopes had been raised by the
formation of a pro-Catholic ministry, only to be
dashed to the ground, first by the death of Canning,
and then by the withdrawal of his followers from
the succeeding ministry. In these circumstances
it was almost inevitable that they should try to
embarrass and intimidate the Government by the
return of a Roman Catholic in defiance of the law

which forbade him to take his seat. It was an open threat that at the next general election the Irish counties would paralyse and discredit the Union by refusing to accept representation on dishonourable terms. Never was a political *coup* better timed or more successful. Against such organised resolution force was worse than useless, and even the army, with its considerable Catholic element, was not wholly to be trusted. Ministers were warned by their own Lord Lieutenant that the maintenance of Protestant ascendancy would lead to rebellion, that a civil war would practically destroy the union of the kingdoms, and that the war, whatever its result, would be a ruinous disaster both to Ireland and to Great Britain. During the winter Peel and Wellington came to certain definite conclusions. The Catholic question could no longer be coquetted with, it must be definitely solved one way or the other. The maintenance of the *status quo* could not be a final solution, and any decision to uphold it involved the country in inevitable disasters. Concession to the Catholics they had always held to be an evil, and they still believed it to be an evil. But in the circumstances it was the lesser evil, and it must be carried in order to avert worse disasters.

The obvious and easy course was to resign and to throw the responsibility of passing the necessary legislation upon the party which had

long advocated it. But this course was ruled out
by present conditions. If concession was to be
of any use, it must be made at once. A Whig-
Canningite ministry could carry a Bill through the
Commons, but they could not possibly surmount
the two great barriers, the House of Lords and the
Crown. Hence the unpleasing but irresistible conclusion that the present ministers should undertake
the distasteful task of repudiating their past pro-
fessions and of forcing upon a recalcitrant party a
measure which they had consistently denounced.
And they had to admit that they yielded, not to
the force of argument, but to agitation stirred up
by the detested O'Connell and to the fear of rebellion. Nothing but the sternest sense of duty
could have induced men to submit to such humiliation. Wellington, with his military training and
his habit of putting duty before all other considerations, could face the unpleasant prospect with
tolerable composure. Peel, far more sensitive by
nature, and conscious of his virtual pledges to his
University constituents, offered to resign on the
plea that he could render more efficient support if
he were outside the ministry. But he knew in his
heart that he could not be dispensed with, and in
the very letter of resignation he intimated that if
his chief thought it necessary for the success of the
cause that he should remain in office, he would do
so. To this there could be only one answer. Peel

remained in office and resigned his seat for Oxford, in spite of reproaches that he thereby admitted a member of parliament to be a delegate.[1] A contest resulted in the return of that model Tory, Sir Robert Inglis. Peel had to fall back on another nomination borough, and as member for Westbury he piloted the Emancipation Bill through the House of Commons. Three sops were thrown to the Tory Cerberus. The Catholic Association was dissolved; the franchise was raised from the forty shilling freeholder to the ten pound householder; and O'Connell was not allowed to take his seat for Clare until he had passed through a second election. These acts of homage to party spirit irritated Ireland, and did no good to anybody; but they helped Wellington to obtain the necessary majority in the Lords. Still the combined and resolute efforts of both the leading ministers were required to overcome what Peel described as the last and most difficult of all obstacles, the resistance of the King.[2] But George IV. was a weak man when properly handled, and the Bill became law.

I have dwelt at some length upon this measure of Catholic emancipation because it was Peel's first breach with party obligations, and it was the most unpleasant and the most courageous act of his whole career. It is to his credit that he found time

[1] For Croker's remonstrances against this " democratical and unconstitutional proceeding " see *Croker Papers*, ii. p. 7.

[2] *Croker Papers*, ii. 14.

and energy in this distasteful session of 1829 to organise that metropolitan police which has attracted the respectful admiration of generations of foreign visitors, and which helped to maintain order in London in marked contrast to the provincial rioting which broke out during the struggle over parliamentary reform.

The year 1830 which followed was a notable epoch in Peel's career. The death of his father gave him the baronetcy and complete pecuniary independence. It made him in fact one of the wealthiest commoners of England, and enabled him to become an enlightened patron of the fine arts. The death of George IV. deprived the Tory party of a substantial, though not a wholly unshakable, bulwark, and transferred the Crown, with its ill-defined but still considerable influence, to a king who was known to have an unreasoned hankering for credit and popularity as a reforming ruler. Finally, the July Revolution in Paris shattered the credit of the English ministry, which was suspected of having sympathies with the reactionary policy of Polignac. The downfall of the Wellington administration, which must anyhow have resulted from Tory division and discontent, was followed by the calling in of Lord Grey and the two years' struggle over successive Reform Bills. If Peel had been the leader of his party he might have taken advantage of the situation to adopt a policy of moderate reform.[1] But the way was barred by Wellington's indiscreet and ill-timed declaration against any change in the representative system, which he declared to possess the entire confidence of the country. Committed by his leader to an attitude of stolid resistance, Peel led the Opposition in the Commons with dignified moderation, but without any hope of ultimate success. In his own words, he wanted " to make the *descensus* as *difficilis* as we can—to teach young inexperienced men charged with the trust of government that, although they may be backed by popular clamour . . . the carrying of extensive changes in the Constitution without previous deliberation shall not be a holiday task . . . that people may hereafter distinguish between the amendment and the over-turning of their institutions ".[2]

There is only one episode in the Reform struggle that requires special notice. In the spring of 1832, when William IV. refused the first demand of the Whig ministers for the creation of peers, the King sent for Lord Lyndhurst, who advised the creation of a Tory ministry to carry a " moderate " Reform Bill. When the King urged that his honour was pledged by the support he had given to the present

[1] Croker wrote to Lord Hertford on January 19, 1831, that Peel refused to pledge himself, like the Duke, against all Parliamentary Reform. " He said, good-humouredly, that he was sick with eating pledges, and would take care to avoid them in the future " (*Croker Papers*, ii. p. 101).

[2] Peel to Lord Harrowby, February 5, 1832, in Parker, ii. p. 201.

F

measure, Lyndhurst agreed that the Bill should
be an "extensive" one. Wellington, with characteristic readiness to subordinate his own professed
convictions, was willing to accept office on these
terms. But Peel, breaking away from the allegiance
which had hitherto hampered him, interposed an
absolute refusal which in the circumstances was a
virtual veto.[1] The reasons for his refusal are
expressed in a letter to Croker, and, in view of his
future conduct, his words are worth quoting :

> I foresee that a Bill of Reform, including everything
> that is really important and dangerous in the present Bill,
> must pass. For me individually to take the conduct of
> such a Bill, would be, in my opinion, personal degradation
> to myself. . . . I look beyond the exigency and the peril
> of the present moment, and I do believe that one of the
> greatest calamities that could befall the country would be
> the utter want of confidence in the declarations of public
> men which must follow the adoption of the Bill of Reform
> by me as a Minister of the Crown. It is *not* a repetition of
> the Catholic question. I was then in office. I had advised
> the concession as a minister. I should now assume office
> for the purpose of carrying the measure to which up to
> the last moment I have been inveterately opposed.[2]

Peel's opinion prevailed, the King's offer was
refused, and it was agreed that, in order to avert,
if possible, the necessity of creating new peers, the

[1] Creevey writes exultantly on May 18, 1832, that the Whig ministers
had reported their retention of office. "This was followed by a most
valuable declaration from Peel that he would never have joined the
late attempted administration of the Duke of Wellington" (*Creevey
Papers*, ii. 246).

[2] Peel to Croker, May 12, 1832, Parker, *Peel*, ii. p. 205.

Duke should withdraw his opposition in the House
of Lords, and so the Reform Bill finally passed.

This episode marks a distinct change in the
relations of the two Tory leaders. There was no
formal recognition of the transfer of authority, but
the firm of Wellington and Peel had obviously
become Peel and Wellington. Interested observers
detected and deplored a certain lack of cordiality
between them. Their relations were not improved
in 1834 by the election of Wellington as Chancellor
of the University of Oxford. Peel's supporters
suggested that the Duke might withdraw in recognition of Peel's superior claims as a graduate and
of his academic distinctions. Wellington, while
admitting his own lack of qualifications, refused to
decline nomination, and Peel refused to be put
up against him, but he not unnaturally felt that
the Duke might have had some communication
with him on the subject. There was nothing of the
nature of a rupture between the two men, and in an
emergency they were ready to co-operate, but in
the intervals they tended to fall apart, in spite of
the attempted mediation of Arbuthnot and Croker.
Peel admitted no control and no necessity for
consultation as to his conduct in the House of
Commons. Nor was Wellington less independent
in the Lords, where the Tory majority not infrequently took steps of which Peel did not conceal
his disapprobation.

For nine years after 1832, with two brief inter-
ruptions, Peel led the Opposition in the Commons.
He began with barely 150 supporters, but after the
General Election of 1835 the minority was very
substantially increased. These years were by no
means the least creditable nor the least happy
period of his life. In spite of the growing reputation
of Lord John Russell, he was confronted by no
equal as a debater in the House. Brougham had
gone to that uneasy career in the House of Lords,
in which he wasted his powers and wrecked his
reputation. Stanley and Graham seceded from the
Whigs in 1834, and were on their way to become
Peel's close allies. Peel's hold upon the House and
his credit in the country steadily increased.

Peel formed in his own mind a clear conception
of his duties as an Opposition leader. He resisted
all temptations to join with the Radical extremists
in harassing the Government. In his own words,
he had no sympathy with these people who " think
that the whole art of conducting a party consists
in eternal fussy manœuvring, and little cunning
schemes for putting a Government in a minority ".[1]
He publicly declared at the outset that he accepted
the Reform Act as a " final and irrevocable settlement ". If ministers proposed measures of which
he approved, such as the reform of the Poor Law
and of Municipal Corporations, he was prepared to

[1] Peel to Arbuthnot, May 27, 1834, in Parker, ii. p. 247.

support them. He had no desire to discredit or supplant them, until he had formed and trained a Conservative party, and until that party had gained the confidence of the country. Ultra-Tories, like the Duke of Newcastle and his former ally, the King of Hanover,[1] might growl at what they considered to be truckling to the spirit of reform, but Peel had finally broken with ultra-Toryism. He expressed himself clearly to Croker :

> The question is not, Can you turn out a Government ? but, Can you keep in any Government, and stave off confusion ? What are we doing at this moment ? We are making the Reform Bill work ; we are falsifying our own predictions, which would be realised but for our active interference ; we are protecting the authors of the evil from the work of their own hands.[2]

This was real statesmanship, though it was bitterly criticised by " crafty and insidious " politicians. And it had its reward. In 1839 a disgruntled Radical declared in the Commons that " the right honourable Member for Tamworth governs England. The honourable and learned Member for Dublin governs Ireland. The Whigs govern nothing but Downing Street." [3]

[1] The King of Hanover (formerly Duke of Cumberland), kept in touch with English politics through Croker, to whom he wrote in 1838 : " Another fatal point has been, and I remark still continues, namely, that the leaders come always to the aid and assistance of ministers when they are in difficulties " (*Croker Papers*, ii. p. 327).

[2] Peel to Croker, March 5, 1833, *ibid.* ii. p. 216.

[3] Quoted from a speech by Leader, Radical Member for Westminster, in a debate on the Irish policy of the Government (Thursfield, *Peel*, p. 163).

The first interruption of Peel's complacent and rather patronising opposition was wholly unexpected and probably equally undesired. Peel himself anticipated it so little that he had gone to Italy with his wife and daughter. The death of Earl Spencer removed his son, Lord Althorp, from the Commons, where he had been the Whig leader under both Lord Grey and Lord Melbourne. On the plea that Lord John Russell was unequal to the task, and that the ministers would be unable to carry on the Government without Lord Althorp's assistance in the Commons, William IV. dismissed Melbourne and his colleagues, from whom he was by this time completely alienated. It has been held that Melbourne had represented the loss of Althorp as a fatal blow to the administration, and that the King was entitled to regard this as a virtual resignation. But William subsequently claimed the change of administration as his own " immediate and exclusive act ",[1] and it was regarded and resented as such by the Whig party. Wellington, who was at once appealed to by the King, was wise enough to decline a second premiership on the plea that the chief minister ought to be in the Commons, and urged the sending for Peel. Pending the latter's return, the Duke undertook to act as interim First Lord of the Treasury and Home Secretary, while the Seal was to be put in commission. The

---

[1] See letter from William IV. to the Cabinet in Parker, ii. p. 288.

" hurried Hudson " was sent post-haste to Italy, and Peel returned with all possible speed to England.

Peel was conscious that the time was not yet ripe for the formation of a Conservative ministry, and he did not consider that the King's action was either judicious or constitutional. But he could not repudiate Wellington's action, and he set himself to make the best of a situation for which he was not responsible. In the hope of constructing his administration on as broad a basis as possible, he made overtures to Stanley and Graham, and he issued the famous Tamworth manifesto, which Lord Lyndhurst said might have been written in Brooks's.[1] But the ex-Whig politicians declined to enter the Cabinet, on the ground that its initiation was due to the action of Wellington, and that this gave it too obvious a Tory tinge. So Peel had to be content with what he querulously described as " only the Duke's old Cabinet ".[2] As he was in a hopeless minority in the first Reform Parliament, he was compelled to resort to a dissolution. The election gave him nearly a hundred additional followers, but he was still in a minority. His last hope was to disarm opposition by the merit and moderation of his measures, but the Whigs, exasperated by the conduct of the King, were in no mood to extend to Peel the consideration which he

[1] *Creevey Papers*, ii. p. 302. The Tamworth letter is conveniently printed in full in Thursfield, *Peel*, pp. 136-142.

[2] *Croker Papers*, ii. p. 249.

had shown to them. An alliance with O'Connell's tail gave them an undisputed superiority of numbers, and they used it without mercy. Defeated on the nomination of a Speaker, on the Address, and in a number of subsequent divisions, Peel admitted the impossibility of conducting the Government in such conditions, and insisted upon resigning. William IV. was compelled to restore the ministers whom he had dismissed, but he grimly declared they should never enjoy his confidence, and that he would receive their advice with jealousy and suspicion. It is easy to understand with what glee the Whig ministers welcomed the accession of Queen Victoria, when Melbourne's courtly and paternal manners gained him such influence with the young Queen that his opponents denounced him as a virtual Mayor of the Palace.

But royal favour, though it made the position of ministers more comfortable, could not make it more secure. They were confronted with ever-increasing difficulties—financial deficits, social discontent and disorder, the unpopularity of the new Poor Law, disturbances in Europe, and serious troubles in the Colonies. What proved in the end one of their best achievements, the sending of Lord Durham to deal with the problems raised by the rebellion in Lower Canada, was at the time a complete fiasco, and Durham was recalled in disgrace. When in 1839 the proposal to withdraw

the constitution of Jamaica was carried by only
five votes, the ministers interpreted this as a virtual
defeat, and resigned. For the second time the
Sovereign sent for Wellington, and for the second
time he recommended the calling in of Peel. On
this occasion Peel had no hesitation or misgivings
about accepting the proffered task, and he had
already prepared a list of his principal colleagues,
including this time Stanley and Graham, when the
enterprise was wrecked on the question of the
Ladies of the Bedchamber. It is needless to dwell
upon so obsolete a problem. The young Queen was,
by her own avowal, not unwilling to show her
dislike of the ministerial change, and was rather
eager to test a royal authority which she had as
yet had no opportunity of exercising. She complained that Peel was " such an odd cold man ",[1]
and even his friends admitted that he was gauche
and ill-at-ease in unfamiliar and uncongenial
surroundings. The most serious part of the episode
was that the Queen was in consultation with
Melbourne behind the scenes, and that the ex-
ministers returned to office by encouraging their
Sovereign to resist a demand which two years later,
under wiser guidance, she admitted to be reasonable.

Peel's return to office was merely delayed by this
misadventure. The two extra years which the
Whig ministers purchased by their complacency

[1] *Letters of Queen Victoria*, i. p. 159.

were years of ever-increasing weakness and humiliation. The inclusion of Macaulay after his return from India gave them an additional orator in the House of Commons, but did little to redress the inequality of debating power. The disputes with Mehemet Ali, which brought the country to the verge of war with France, excited misgivings as to Palmerston's wisdom and caution. But the chief trouble was discontent at home. As a last effort to regain their lost popularity, they resolved to meddle with the Corn Laws, and to suggest a moderate fixed duty in place of the current sliding scale which had operated since 1828. But they excited more alarm than they conciliated support. It was said that they had made the Lichfield House compact with Irish repealers, and now they were truckling to the agitators of the Anti-Corn Law League. And they clung to office with far greater tenacity than they had shown in 1839. Even a hostile majority of thirty-eight on the question of the sugar duties could not drive them to resign. At last Peel in person forced an issue by proposing a direct want of confidence, and the vote was carried by a majority of one. Still the ministry would not resign, but appealed to the country, where they met with an electoral disaster comparable to that which overwhelmed Fox's martyrs in 1784. Peel had at last the conservative majority for which he had waited and worked (1841).

Peel's great administration—Bagehot called it
" the most intelligent Conservative Government
that this country has ever seen "—only lasted for
four, or if the prolongation be included, for five
years. In that period it accomplished very substantial work, in striking contrast to the comparatively barren period of the later Whig years.
And by universal consent the chief credit for this
work must be given to Peel himself. Many of his
colleagues were men of real ability and distinction,
but the Prime Minister stood head and shoulders
above them. And Peel was more definitely *Prime*
Minister than most of his predecessors, and probably than any of his successors. Walpole may
have possessed equal authority, but he gained it
by the exclusion of all able and possible rivals.
Chatham at his greatest was even more dictatorial
in all matters that touched on the war, but there
were departments with which he did not meddle.
Pitt's power was exceptional, but he could not
dictate to Grenville, and he had to yield to his
colleagues in dealing with the settlement with
Russia in 1791. To the efficiency and thorough-
ness of Peel's supervision of all departments Mr.
Gladstone, one of his ablest colleagues, has borne
unimpeachable testimony. The exhausting labour
which this involved probably undermined Peel's
naturally robust constitution, and this must be
borne in mind when we come to the crucial years

1845 and 1846. Two simple facts illustrate Peel's ascendancy in these years. His most eminent colleague, Wellington, debarred by age and increasing deafness from holding office, sat in the Cabinet without a portfolio and cheerfully undertook the duty of piloting through the Upper House whatever measures Peel sent up from the Commons. His Chancellor of the Exchequer, Henry Goulburn, was a financier of experience and ability, but he had to stand on one side while Peel introduced and conducted all the vitally important fiscal reforms. And if Peel was autocratic in his Cabinet, he was almost equally so in the House of Commons. On one occasion a hostile amendment on the sugar duties was carried against him by thirty-seven votes. Apologetic rebels pleaded that it was a small matter, and showed no want of confidence in the Government. Peel would accept no excuses, and insisted on a reversal of the decision. In spite of a mutinous protest by Disraeli, the docile house submitted by a majority of twenty-one.

Peel had one great advantage over his predecessors in that Wellington's devotion freed him from all serious opposition in the House of Lords. On the other hand he inherited from them a very difficult and in some respects a dangerous condition of affairs. With the external difficulties—in India and Canada, with France and the United States—the new ministers grappled with a fair measure of

success. But the two problems which attracted
Peel's closest attention were Ireland and finance,
and under the latter head the Corn Laws had been
forced into sudden prominence, partly by the
agitation led by Cobden and Bright, but mainly
by the recent conversion of the Whig leaders to a
fixed duty of eight shillings. It was this which
had bulked most largely in the general election,
and had contributed to the ruinous defeat of the
party. The Free Traders would not have their duty,
and the Tories would not allow them to tamper
with the sacred protection of agriculture.

In Ireland trouble revived because O'Connell,
freed from his compact with the Whigs by their
downfall, now openly raised the standard of
Repeal. Peel met the demand with the usual
mixture of coercion and concession. On the one
hand an Arms Bill and the prosecution of
O'Connell; on the other a trebling of the grant to
Maynooth for the education of priests, an honourable
insistence that Catholic emancipation should be
carried out in the spirit as well as in the letter of the
law,[1] and the endowment of three Queen's Colleges

[1] See Peel's letter to Lord De Grey of August 22, 1843 (Parker,
iii. p. 56), in which he contends that it is not sufficient ground for
rejecting a Roman Catholic candidate for office to say that there is a
superior Protestant in the field. The Protestants, he says, owe their
superiority to their long monopoly of privilege, and if they are allowed
to retain this, the equality granted by law becomes a dead letter. To
Graham he wrote confidentially (*ibid.* p. 53), " We must *look out* for
respectable Roman Catholics for office ". This represents a marked
advance from Peel's original hostility to the Catholic claims.

for the provision of non-sectarian education. On
the Maynooth Bill, which drove Gladstone from the
Cabinet, Peel fought a prolonged and highly creditable fight against the embittered prejudices of
both Englishmen and Scotsmen, and Lord Morley
pronounces it to have been the boldest act of his
career.[1]

But it is Peel's fiscal measures that have been
rightly regarded, both by contemporaries and by
posterity, as his supreme achievement. To the
Bank Act, which narrowly restricted the issue of
bank notes, I have already alluded. It has been
adversely criticised on the ground that it has
failed to prevent panics, and that when they have
occurred it has been found necessary to suspend its
operation. But in this last fact lies its real justification. Its restrictions have inspired such absolute confidence in the note issue of the Bank of
England, that their suspension, or even the report
of an intention to suspend them, has sufficed to
restore confidence and to avert disaster. The other
great measures were the two famous budgets of
1842 and 1845. It is difficult in the present day
to feel any great enthusiasm over the revival of
the income tax, which has been with us from that
day to this. Pitt had instituted it as a supreme
instrument of war. Peel restored it as a necessary

---

[1] *Life of Gladstone*, i. p. 270, " It was one of the boldest things he
ever did " ; *Life of Cobden*, i. p. 326, " Nothing that he ever did showed
greater courage than the Maynooth Grant ".

basis of fiscal reform. In 1842 a tax of 7d. in the
pound was imposed for three years. The revenue
which it brought in enabled him to clear off the
deficits bequeathed by the Whigs, to lower the
sliding scale on the import of corn, and to abolish
or reduce a large number of customs duties, especially those on raw materials and partially manu-
factured articles. Three years later the tax was
renewed in order to carry still further the enfranchisement of trade.

From the outset Peel recognised that the economic arguments for freeing the import of manu-
factures were equally applicable to agricultural
produce, and that in pure theory the Corn Laws
were indefensible. Cobden wrote exultantly to
his brother in the summer of 1842 that " Peel is a
Free-trader, and so are Ripon and Gladstone ".[1]
But at the moment Peel refused to admit that the
economic argument was in itself sufficient to decide
the question. He sought to remove the misgivings
of Croker by a long letter in July 1842, of which
the following is the most important paragraph.

We do not push this argument to its logical consequences—namely that wheat should be at 35s. instead of
50s. or 54s. We take into account vested interests,
engaged capital, the importance of independent supply,
the social benefits of flourishing agriculture. We find the
general welfare will be best promoted by a fair adjustment,
by allowing the legitimate logical deductions to be con-

[1] Morley's *Cobden*, i. p. 242.

trolled by the thousand considerations which enter into moral and political questions, and which, as friction and the weight of the atmosphere, put a limit to the practical application of abstract reasoning.[1]

Croker seems to have been reassured by Peel's insistence upon political and social considerations. But a more impartial correspondent might have foreseen that these considerations would give way if some strong counterbalancing argument should present itself. This was furnished three years later by the disastrous failure of the Irish potato crop. This convinced Peel that famine could be averted only by opening the ports, and he could not conscientiously assure his supporters that, once opened, they could be closed again. He submitted these considerations to the Cabinet in October and November, but the majority, including Wellington and Stanley, shrank from a sudden reversal of the protectionist policy to which they were virtually pledged by the assurances given in the election of 1841. While this deadlock continued, Lord John Russell issued the famous Edinburgh letter of November 27, in which he declared for the repeal of the Corn Laws. This letter acted partly as a curb and partly as a spur to Peel. On the one hand, to announce his own conversion, as yet carefully concealed from the public, would

[1] Peel to Croker, August 3, 1742, in Parker, i. p. 530. The whole letter, with its predecessor on July 27, is worth reading. Both are also printed in the *Croker Papers*, ii. 384-6.

savour of a servile following of his opponent's lead. On the other hand, the repeal was now virtually assured, and it was not attractive to allow all the credit to be gained by the Whig leader. The spur was the more operative, and Peel now submitted to his colleagues a more definite proposal for a gradual extinction of the corn duties accompanied by counterbalancing concessions to the agricultural interests. This time, in view of the altered situation, there was less opposition, but the Duke of Buccleuch and Lord Stanley remained obdurate. Stanley's resistance was the more serious because in the previous year he had received a peerage in order to assist Wellington in the Upper House, and it was in the Lords that the greatest difficulties were expected.

Peel was chagrined at this unwonted opposition within his own Cabinet. As he had declared that he could not proceed unless his colleagues were unanimous, he insisted upon resigning, and the Queen, now as reluctant to part with her minister as she had previously been to accept him, had to send for Lord John Russell. After demanding, and receiving through Peel, an assurance that the avowed Protectionists were not prepared to take office, Russell accepted the royal commission to form a ministry. A few days later he threw it up on the paltry excuse that Lord Grey (the son of the Reform Bill premier) had refused to enter the

Cabinet if Palmerston returned to the Foreign
Office, and that Palmerston would accept no other
post. The Queen cheerfully recalled Peel who, in
an outburst of loyalty worthy of Wellington in his
prime, replied that he would be her minister happen
what may, and that he would do without a colleague rather than leave her in this extremity.
He at once reassembled his Cabinet, and all his
colleagues, with the exception of Stanley, agreed to
follow the leader, under whose banner they had
served for four eventful years. Stanley's place
was filled by the return to office of Gladstone, who
was, unfortunately, without a seat in the Commons.
His assistance would have been invaluable in the
stormy session which followed. Peel may have
hoped for a moment that he would find his party
as docile as his fellow-ministers. If so, he was
woefully disabused by the widespread revolt which
was promptly organised by Lord George Bentinck
and Disraeli. The story of the session has been
told for all time by one of the great protagonists in
the drama. In the young Jew, whose proffered
services Peel had deliberately declined, he met
with a master of flouts and gibes, under which
his proud and sensitive nature suffered acutely.
But he maintained his cause with all his old courage
and tenacity, and he won a complete though
costly victory. His analysis of the final division,
which he transmitted to the Queen on February 28,

1846, is worth recording: "Government, 112; Whigs and Radicals, 227; Protectionists, 231; Whig Protectionists, 11." This meant that of their normal supporters the ministers could only poll less than a third, whereas more than two-thirds actually voted against them. In addition the absentees were also to be reckoned as malcontents. Prince Albert made the obvious comment in reply that 112 certain supporters out of 658 did not look like a strong Government.[1]

As a matter of fact the Government was doomed. Wellington, whose wrath was roused by what he regarded as " the abominable combination " against Peel, rendered his last service to his old colleague by procuring a majority of 47 for the Corn Bill in the House of Lords. On the very same evening (June 25, 1846) that this welcome news arrived, the ministry was defeated by a majority of 73 on the second reading of their Coercion Bill for Ireland.

Party spirit thus wreaked a deliberate vengeance upon the man who had presumed to defy it. Both Bentinck and Disraeli had approved of the Coercion Bill on its introduction. They knew it to be necessary for the maintenance of order, and that necessity was demonstrated by the action of the succeeding ministry, but they determined on a purely factious combination with Whigs and

---

[1] Parker, iii. p. 342.

Repealers for the sole purpose of punishing Peel.
Lord John Russell defended the conduct of his
momentary allies as being the result of a natural
resentment against the man who had twice betrayed his supporters. The defence has been accepted by party politicians, but to the non-political
mind the method by which the Protectionist rebels
wreaked their revenge will always appear to have
been a dastardly act.

On the next day, June 26, the Cabinet met. It
is not often that we are allowed to penetrate the
veil of secrecy which is supposed to shroud a
Cabinet meeting. But Mr. Gladstone himself has
drawn an account of this historic scene. With
characteristic reserve, Peel had given no hint of
his intentions, and it was known that Wellington
was pugnaciously prepared to carry on. But the
authority of the great chief was still unquestioned.

It was the shortest Cabinet I ever knew. Peel himself
uttered two or three introductory sentences. He then said
that he was convinced that the formation of a Conservative
party was impossible while he continued in office. That
he had made up his mind to resign. That he strongly
advised the resignation of the entire Government. Some
declared their assent. None objected ; and when he asked
whether it was unanimous, there was no voice in the
negative.

In another note Gladstone added :

The Duke in my opinion was right and Peel was wrong,
but he had borne the brunt of battle already beyond the

measure of human strength, and who can wonder that his heart and soul as well as his physical organisation needed rest ? [1]

Peel himself never doubted that he did right in resigning. His own attitude is clearly described in a letter to Sir Henry Hardinge, then Governor-General in India, the one political colleague to whom he wrote not only with confidence, but with obvious affection.

So far from regretting the expulsion from office, I rejoice in it as the greatest relief from an intolerable burden. To have your own way, and to be for five years the minister of this country in the House of Commons is quite enough for any man's strength. He is entitled to his discharge, from length of service. But to have to incur the deepest responsibility, to bear the heaviest toil, to reconcile colleagues with conflicting opinions to a common course of action, to keep together in harmony the Sovereign, the Lords, and the Commons ; to have to do all these things, and to be at the same time the tool of a party— that is to say to adopt the opinions of men who have not had access to your knowledge, and could not profit by it if they had, who spend their time in eating and drinking, and hunting, shooting, gambling, horse-racing, and so forth—would be an odious servitude to which I never will submit. I intend to keep aloof from party combinations. So far as a man can be justified in forming such a resolution, I am determined not again to resume office. . . . I will take care not again to burn my fingers by organising a party. There is too much truth in the saying " The head of a party must be directed by the tail ". As heads see,

---

[1] Morley, *Life of Gladstone*, i. p. 290.

and tails are blind, I think heads the best judges as to the course to be taken.[1]

Peel had at last broken away from the party system. In the speech in which he intimated his resignation, he emphasised and confirmed his repudiation of party ties by attributing the chief credit for the repeal of the Corn Laws to Richard Cobden, the man who from innumerable platforms had so bitterly denounced the landlord class. Even Mr. Gladstone, of all public men the most akin to Peel by birth and training, deplored and even resented this slur upon his immediate supporters. But Peel refused to retract or to modify what he had said. When he quitted office, he was unquestionably, after the Duke of Wellington, the most eminent subject of the Crown. But without a party, he was, like Chatham in not dissimilar conditions, a political outcast. Even an alliance with the Whigs, if he could have contemplated such an act, could not have restored to him the authority he had enjoyed and lost. For the last four years of his life he was an honoured spectator of the political drama. He kept his seat in the Commons, he could always secure an attentive hearing in

[1] Peel to Hardinge, September 24, 1846, in Parker, iii. p. 473. Compare Peel's letter to his wife in December 1845, written in anticipation of Tory denunciation (*Private Letters*, p. 273). " How can those, who spend their time in hunting and shooting and eating and drinking, know what were the motives of those who are responsible for the public security, who have access to the best information, and have no other object under Heaven but to provide against danger, and consult the general interest of all classes ? "

the House and the country, but he could do no more than give a discriminating support to the politicians who had displaced him. He did not like the foreign policy of Palmerston, but he agreed with Graham, " that Palmerston and his foreign policy are less to be dreaded than Stanley and a new Corn Law ".[1] It was largely due to Peel, and after his death to the little band of Peelites, that Protection became, in Disraeli's phrase, " not only dead but damned ". Peel supported the repeal of the Navigation Acts, which was in a sense the completion of his own work. He had the satisfaction of seeing the British crown and constitution stand proudly erect amidst the shattering storms of 1848, and of knowing that his own measures had contributed to their stability. When his life was prematurely closed in 1850 by the accident on Constitution Hill, the nation, in the simple words of Queen Victoria, mourned over him as over a father.[2]

Lady Peel refused the peerage offered to her by the Queen on the ground that her husband had expressly desired that no member of his family should accept any title or distinction in recognition of his services, but only if they earned such a reward for themselves. Sir Robert's descendants have honourably carried out his injunction.

[1] Graham to Peel, April 3, 1850, in Parker, iii. p. 536.
[2] Queen Victoria to the King of the Belgians, July 9, 1850 (*Letters*, ii. p. 256).

III

Looking back upon Peel's career, one may venture on certain obvious comments. He entered political life with what appeared to be overwhelming advantages. His father's wealth and generosity freed him from all sordid pecuniary troubles and temptations. He had himself magnificent personal endowments : prodigious industry (it was quite superfluous for the Dean of Christ Church to urge him to " work like a tiger "), a power of rapid and thorough assimilation, and a memory that has been compared to that of Macaulay. He had a fine presence and a beautiful speaking voice, only equalled in that generation, says Disraeli, by O'Connell's resonant organ. He was no orator, in the sense of swaying mobs, but he had an unfailing command of fluent, orderly, and convincing speech, probably the best style of oratory for a deliberative assembly. The shyness, which made him appear awkward and reserved in social life, and which prevented him from ever mastering what Lord Rosebery calls the " Tom, Dick, and Harry style " with his supporters, never affected him in the House of Commons, where he was from the first completely at home. He was associated by education and social habits with the class which had dominated England since the Restoration, and the game bags which he complacently chronicled in his letters to his wife prove that he was proficient in at least one of the accepted recreations of a country gentleman. The race-course he left to his brother Jonathan, and in the hunting-field he was never conspicuous. The Whigs, who nick-named him " Spinning Jenny ", did their best to discredit him in the eyes of his aristocratic associates, but the legend that the latter slighted him and that he avenged the slights by attacking the agricultural interest was long ago refuted by Disraeli and is fully contradicted by Peel's private letters. It was not until the gentry denounced his political actions that he retaliated by condemning the intellectual equipment of those who spent their life in eating and drinking, hunting, shooting, and horse-racing. Until that time he associated with them on easy and familiar terms, and they were glad enough to get him to shoot their covers.

Peel's political promotion was extraordinarily rapid. His brilliant academic reputation, less common and more highly valued in those days than now, secured for him an interested hearing in the House. He entered, by acquiescence rather than by choice, a party which seemed, by its conduct of the war to a triumphant conclusion, to have secured a lasting monopoly of office. And this party was not so well supplied with able and eloquent champions that it could afford to give anything but a warm welcome to so valuable a recruit. Within a year an official post was found for him. Before he was thirty-four years old he had twice refused Cabinet rank. When, at that age, he entered the Cabinet, it was as one of His Majesty's Principal Secretaries of State. And within a year he was seriously regarded, and was actually supported by the King, as a rival of Canning for the leadership of the House of Commons.

And yet, from another point of view, there were drawbacks to this apparent good fortune. Peel had been trained for politics : he had yet to get his training in politics. It was impossible for a youth, hitherto immersed at school and college in the study of classics and mathematics, to have more than a superficial grasp of political principles or political aims. He accepted his father's politics just as he accepted his father's gift of a seat in Parliament. And he was prematurely captured by the party—one tradition says deliberately captured in order to prevent his threatened escape—by his immediate admission to official place and duties. Nor was this the only misfortune. If his promotion had been delayed, he would have had time to find his own political place without attracting undue attention. But a man who is engaged in the actual hurly-burly of active politics cannot sit down and think out his own opinions *in vacuo* like a professor in his study.

He is perpetually influenced, and in large measure guided, by his surroundings. Personal friendships, and still more personal antagonisms, play a great part in shaping his opinions. This was conspicuously the case with Peel. His early collision with O'Connell did much to harden his views on the Irish and the Catholic question. But I attach far more importance to his relations with Canning.

The Tory party, when Peel joined it, had, as parties usually have, a left and a right wing. On the left the leader was the brilliant figure of George Canning, whom the orthodox Tories on the right regarded with growing mistrust and reprobation. They were naturally eager to find some one to pit against him, and they thought they had found their man in Robert Peel. There was no personal animosity or vulgar jealousy between the two men, but circumstances combined to pull them apart. On the great question of the day they took opposite sides. It was Canning's intense ambition to represent his University : the choice of Oxford fell upon Peel.[1] In 1822 it required all Canning's ability and determination to avoid going to India, and to defeat the efforts to secure the leadership in the Commons for Peel. In 1827 he found Peel opposed to his promotion to the premiership, and

[1] Lord Holland to Creevey, June 24, 1817: "Peel's election has galled the Cannings to the quick" (*Creevey Papers*, i. p. 263). Canning never concealed his disappointment.

when he had gained it, Peel refused to enter his Cabinet. In all this Canning admitted that Peel's personal conduct was irreproachable ; but there could be no doubt that the younger man was, in the eyes of contemporaries, his rival and in some measure his opponent.[1]

All this tended to identify Peel with the right wing of the Tory party, and to bring him into close association with two men who undoubtedly exercised a great influence over his career and for a time over his opinions. These men were the Duke of Wellington and John Wilson Croker. Of his relations with Wellington I have already spoken. Croker has been too harshly judged by a generation which knows him only through the diatribes of Macaulay and from the malicious portrait of Rigby in the pages of *Coningsby*. He was unquestionably a man of wide interests, of notable ability, and of deserved political weight. The three volumes of his *Correspondence and Diaries* will always be, like the Journal of Charles Greville, an invaluable commentary on the history of the first half of the nineteenth century. And by far the most interesting and important letters in these volumes are those which passed between himself

[1] Disraeli says (Lord George Bentinck, p. 286), "Those who are well informed of the political history of the country, know that between Mr. Canning and Mr. Peel there existed an antipathy. They disliked each other ; Mr. Canning was jealous of Mr. Peel, and Mr. Peel was a little envious of Mr. Canning."

and Peel. There can be no doubt that Croker and
Wellington, both real Tories, acted as a restraint
upon Peel's political development. The extent of
Croker's influence is to be measured by the acute-
ness of the final rupture in 1846. There is something more than resentment at a temporary mis-
judgment of motives in Peel's final repudiation of
the Croker influence. Few men can have received
such a slap in the face as was given to Croker in
the last letter of a man who for more than a generation had addressed him as " My dear Croker ", and
had signed himself " yours affectionately ".

I trust there is nothing inconsistent with perfect
civility in the expression of an earnest wish that the same
principle which suggests to you the propriety of closing a
written correspondence of seven and thirty years, may be
extended to every other species of intercourse.[1]

Peel's enfranchisement came strangely late.
There can be no doubt that the Wellington-Croker
influence, like the earlier involuntary antagonism
to Canning, kept Peel nominally within the Tory
fold long after he ought to have quitted it. For
it is clear that Peel was never really a Tory in any
sense of that much misunderstood term, and still
less at a time when Toryism had been petrified by
repulsion from the French Revolution into an un-

---

[1] *Croker Papers*, iii. p. 94. There had been in 1827 a previous
rupture between Peel and Croker, on account of the latter's relations
with Canning during the ministerial crisis which followed Lord Liverpool's
breakdown. See Parker, i. pp. 469-73.

reasoning antagonism to all organic reform.[1] Lord
Rosebery seems to think that if Peel had not been
committed by paternal influence, by early training,
and by Lord Liverpool's patronage, to the Tories,
he might have bathed with the Whigs instead of
purloining their empty clothes. This is highly
questionable. With the aristocratic side of Whig-
gism he had no real sympathy, and he had an instinctive antipathy to Radicalism, with its appeal
to the constituents and the head of their representatives. He was really a misfit in the party
system. He would have made an ideal first
minister to a benevolent despot, who might have
safely commissioned him to rule, without regard
to class or privilege, in the interests of the security
of the State and of the welfare of the great mass
of its members. Or he might have been, what
Cobden desired him to become, the leader of a
great middle party, holding the balance between
two opposing extremes, and appealing for support
to moderate and reasonable men.[2] But English
tradition does not admit of middle parties, except
for a brief and transitory period. The Peelites,

[1] The Duke of Newcastle, who may be taken as a typical ultra-
Tory, wrote to Peel as late as 1835 : " I would yield nothing to the
spirit of reform, innovation, by whatever name it may be called. It is
because, in my view of the case, concession leads to revolution, that I
would, directly or indirectly, concede nothing " (Parker, ii. 296). The
Duke obviously disapproved of the Tamworth manifesto.

[2] Cobden wrote to his brother on March 22, 1842 : " Peel must head
a *milieu* party soon. If the old Duke were dead, he would quarrel
with the ultra-Tories in a month " (Morley's *Cobden*, i. p. 241).

brilliant and able men as they were, were soon
dispersed, either by death or by absorption in one
or the other of the recognised parties.

IV

Mr. Gladstone used to say that there were two
Peels, one before and one after the Reform Act.[1]
Lord Rosebery expands this statement by saying
that before 1832 Peel was a Tory, and after that
date he was a Whig. As I read it, there are four
clearly defined periods in Peel's career. In the
first, down to 1818, he was an acquiescent Tory,
without any serious inward questionings. But
during his three years' abstention from office he had
more time for reflection and study. In 1819 he
struck his first blow for independence when he
opposed his father's views on the return to cash
payments. In 1820 he wrote a remarkable letter
to Croker in which he expressed an uneasy sense
that public opinion was becoming more liberal than
the policy of the Government; that it would be
impossible to resist for long the demand for reform;
and that he would not be surprised to see a union
of Tories and Whigs to carry out a moderate policy
in resistance to the Hobhouses, Burdetts, and
Radicalism.[2] The letter shows a notable distrust

[1] Parker, i. p. 209.
[2] *Croker Papers*, i. p. 170. Mr. Parker has not included this
interesting letter, although he has inserted a good many of the letters
between Peel and Croker.

of mere negative resistance to change. The process
of emancipation was carried still further during the
years 1822 to 1827, when Peel was associated with
the foreign policy of Canning, and the fiscal policy
of Huskisson. Creevey, a malicious but acute
observer, wrote in 1825 : " Unhappily for Toryism,
that prig Peel seems as deeply bitten by ' liberality '
in every way but on the Catholic question, as
any of his fellows ".[1] Peel's Oxford friends were
seriously alarmed when he declared more than once
that there was only one question which separated
him from Canning.[2] And Canning himself gave
the same disquieting assurance.[3]

Then came the events of 1827 and 1828 which
for nearly five years threw Peel into dependence
upon Wellington, and forced him to become the
advocate of a more negative policy than had
become congenial to him. But during the struggle
for reform he gradually regained his freedom, and
in 1832 the final passing of the Bill altered his whole
situation. It is one of the anomalies of his career
that he was more at home in the Reform Parliaments, whose introduction he had opposed, than he
had been in the earlier assemblies. It was not till
after 1832 that he displayed to the full the qualities

---

[1] *The Creevey Papers*, vol. ii. p. 100.

[2] He said this in 1822 in a private letter to the Speaker (Parker,
i. p. 332). He repeated it to Lord Eldon (*ibid.* p. 460), and to Canning
himself in 1827 (*ibid.* p. 468). The Oxford dissatisfaction was expressed
by Bishop Lloyd to Peel on April 22, 1827 (*ibid.* p. 479).

[3] *Ibid.* p. 465.

which induced Disraeli to call him " the greatest
Member of Parliament that ever lived ".[1]   It must
be remembered that, while Harrow and Christ
Church and a love of shooting attached him to the
great houses and to the country gentry, his ancestry
and his own business acumen entitled him to the
confidence of that mercantile class, which had
exerted considerable influence in the eighteenth
century, and became after 1832 the dominant
political force in the country.   It was their growing
confidence and support which enabled Peel to gain
ascendancy, not as a Whig, or as a Tory, but as a
Conservative Reformer.   So far as he was supported
by the Tories, it was only because he stood between
them and something worse.

There are two episodes in Peel's career about
which there always has been, and always will be,
acute controversy.   Down to 1829 Peel had been
chiefly known as the strongest and ablest opponent
of Catholic emancipation.   It was in that character
that he had been chosen to represent his university.
George IV. wrote to him in 1825 as " the King's
Protestant minister ".[2]   In 1827 he broke with
Canning on this question.   And yet, in 1829 he
himself introduced and carried, with the help of
opposition votes, the very measure which he had
so long and so consistently opposed.   Was he

---

[1] *Lord George Bentinck* (1852), p. 320.
[2] Parker, vol. i. p. 370.

justified in doing this ? Again, in 1841, he was
raised to the premiership as the leader of a party
which had gained a majority at the election as
being in favour of the protection of agriculture.
In 1846 he, remaining Prime Minister, and in the
same Parliament, carried the repeal of the Corn
Laws, again by the support of the Opposition, and
against the votes of more than two-thirds of his
own supporters. Was he justified in doing this ?
These two great acts of apostacy, as they have been
called, are frequently bracketed together, as if
both raised the same problem. There is, of course,
a great gulf between them. In 1829 Peel was *not*
a convert to Catholic relief. In 1846 he *was* a
convinced Free Trader. But in both cases he acted
against previous assurances, either actual or implied,
and in both cases he acted against his own party.

On the general question of political consistency,
Mr. Gladstone has summed up in terms which would
probably meet with almost universal acceptance :

Change of opinion in those to whose judgment the
public looks more or less to assist its own, is an evil to the
country, although a much smaller evil than the persistence
in a course which they know to be wrong. It is not
always to be blamed. But it is always to be watched with
vigilance ; always to be challenged and put upon its trial.[1]

In putting Peel's inconsistency on its trial, Lord
Rosebery has pronounced an adverse verdict. He

[1] Quoted from *Gleanings*, vii. p. 100, in Morley's *Gladstone*, i. p. 211.

thinks—or did think, when he himself was a party politician [1]—that Peel should have given Wellington no chance to keep him in office in 1829, and that in 1845 he should have persisted in his resignation, and so forced Russell to take office, whether with or without Lord Grey. I find it impossible to accept this positive conclusion, which seems to rest upon two dubious assumptions. It assumes that Wellington would have been able to overcome the opposition of the Lords and the Crown to Catholic emancipation if his ministry had been fatally weakened, as it would have been, by Peel's withdrawal. His support as a private member would have been no equivalent for his retention as leader in the Commons. And it also assumes that Russell would have been able to carry through the Repeal of the Corn Laws. But this was effected by the aid of 112 Conservative votes, which were given to keep Peel in office. It is extremely doubtful whether these votes, or the majority of them, would have been given to Russell. And the measure was carried in the Lords by the influence of Wellington. Would he have rendered, and would he have been willing to render, the same service to the Whigs which he did, not without misgivings, render to Peel ?

[1] Lord Rosebery's brilliant estimate of Peel, to which I have been much indebted, originally appeared in the *Anglo-Saxon Review*, was published by Cassell & Co. as a booklet in 1899, and has been reprinted in *Miscellanies* (1921), vol. i.

As to Catholic relief, it seems to stand in a category by itself. It was not a conversion or a change of opinion. It was a deliberate decision to accept an evil in order to avoid a greater evil, and can only be judged on a thorough-going examination of the situation in Ireland at the time. Of course it may be urged that Peel ought not to have opposed emancipation, and thus delayed the concession till it was too late to have any conciliatory effect, and only encouraged agitation and resistance as a means of obtaining redress. In mitigation it may be pointed out that concession never has succeeded in conciliating Ireland, and that it is purely conjectural to maintain that Catholic emancipation in 1825 would have been more successful than it proved in 1829. It must be remembered that Peel's opposition was not based upon religious bigotry, but upon purely political considerations. He believed that the maintenance of the Protestant establishment in Ireland was necessary for the retention of the Union. He held that concession of the Catholic demands would destroy the establishment, and that this would sooner or later be fatal to the Union. It is difficult, in view of later events, to deny the soundness of his reasoning. Peel has often been blamed for a lack of foresight, and an excessive concentration upon the needs of the moment. In this particular case his anticipation of the future seems to have been more clear-sighted than that of his opponents, who urged that Catholic relief would stabilise the Union.

If subsequent experience has provided some defence for Peel's reluctance to grant Catholic emancipation, I suppose it has also justified his conversion to Free Trade. At any rate his policy has been persisted in, in spite of the disappointing reluctance of other countries, including our own Dominions, to follow our lead, and all attempts to reverse this policy have been so far conclusively rejected.

There is, however, one point to be made with regard to the two outstanding episodes of Peel's career, which has not hitherto, so far as I know, been brought into prominence. In both may be detected some element of that masterful self-confidence and that love of autocracy which always characterised Peel, which accounts for a good deal of that reserve of which colleagues and supporters complained, and which undoubtedly grew upon him in his later years. In his own *Memoir* he half admits this with regard to Catholic emancipation : [1]

It may be that I was unconsciously influenced by motives less perfectly pure and disinterested, by the secret satisfaction of being,

> when the waves ran high
> A daring pilot in extremity.

and the same sort of motive was undoubtedly

[1] Quoted in Parker, ii. p. 108.

stronger in 1845–46. He had made up his mind to make a final settlement of the Corn Law question; he had the plan clearly in his head; he knew that he could do it, and probably believed that he could do it better than anybody else, and he was not insensible to, nor quite willing to surrender, the credit which would accrue to the man who cheapened the food of the people. In a letter to Hardinge, written just after his downfall, he uttered the exultant but not discreditable boast: " I pique myself on never having proposed anything that I have not carried ".[1] There spoke the masterful man.

Whatever may be the verdict upon the two hotly disputed actions of Peel, there can be no doubt as to his pre-eminence in his generation or of the value of his services to the country. He did more than any other man to put an end to the distress and depression which followed the Napoleonic Wars, and to lay firm foundations for the material prosperity which characterised the age of Queen Victoria. I am inclined to think that Peel and Palmerston were, in their different spheres, the truest representatives of the prevalent spirit of Victorian England, more truly representative than Disraeli and Gladstone. Peel's services have generally been summed up in terms of legislative enactments. With regard to these he is admitted to

[1] Peel to Hardinge, July 4, 1846; *ibid*. iii. p. 471.

have been rather an assimilator than an originator. Romilly, Horner, Mackintosh, Huskisson, Canning, Cobden—he plagiarised ideas from all of them. Where he excelled was in putting these ideas into a practicable and acceptable shape. What other statesman could say that he had proposed nothing that he did not pass ?

But Peel was not only a legislator. It is one of the weak points of the party system that it concentrates excessive attention on additions to the Statute Book. In many ways administration is more vitally important to the State than legislation. And in this department Peel was unsurpassed. Mr. Gladstone said that he was the best man of business that ever held the office of Prime Minister. He found an administrative system which was crippled by corrupt and restricted patronage. He struck boldly at all corruption, direct and indirect, and he bequeathed to later generations the tradition of pure, honest, and efficient administration. It was perhaps a greater bequest than freedom of trade or even the police force.

I may perhaps be allowed to conclude with a somewhat irrelevant and perhaps improper peroration. We, as the result of the Great War, are passing through a period of difficulty and depression —even greater difficulties than those of Peel's time. We have a Prime Minister, also educated at Harrow, who, though the accepted leader of a party, has admitted that he was raised to office to discharge a national rather than a party service. He could have no greater or more inspiring example than that of Sir Robert Peel.

VISCOUNT PALMERSTON

From a drawing by George Richmond, R.A.
*Reproduced by permission from " Prime Ministers of Great Britain ' by the
Hon. Clive Bigham.* (John Murray.)

LORD PALMERSTON

By PHILIP GUEDALLA

I

I HAVE been so much more often among the lectured than among the lecturers that you will perhaps permit me a moment of sober rejoicing at the unaccustomed position in which I find myself this afternoon. To be invited to lecture in this College is a high privilege for any man, highest of all for a man who has tried to learn history, has tried, indeed, to write history, but has never in his moments of wildest self-esteem pretended to teach history. And I value it the more as an encouragement to proceed with the work—I hope with the last year of work—on a Life of Lord Palmerston, which has mainly filled such parts of the last four years as remained to me after contesting parliamentary elections in what I will openly defy our Chairman [1] by calling the Palmerstonian interest.

And if I may name a further cause of satisfaction,

it is his presence in the chair, not merely because we congratulate him respectfully on the physical achievement of having got here from Westminster, —although that, in view of the maelstroms of rotating traffic, with which he has enlivened the solitary existences of the Metropolitan Police, is a considerable triumph of mind over matter—but because he is so obviously the right person to be here. It is singularly fitting that our proceedings should be directed by the present owner of Broadlands and the son of Mr. Evelyn Ashley, whose work is the foundation of our knowledge of Palmerston. Indeed, if there is one thing more obvious, it is that he ought to be delivering this lecture and I ought to be filling a busy note-book somewhere in front. My only consolation for this irregular proceeding is the opportunity which it affords me to thank him in public, rather than in the relative obscurity of a preface, for the generosity with which he has admitted a total and intrusive stranger to Lord Palmerston's papers; because it is to our Chairman that I owe what is, on the technical side, the main value of such work as I have been able to do—the fact that I have been able to found it on some study of the Broadlands Papers. There could have been no greater aid to the reconstruction of that great figure and the age in which he lived.

I take it, without begging too many questions, that some such reconstruction as that is the main

object of history.   It is an object that is too often
forgotten, because most of those whom we follow
in these matters appear to be so absorbed in the
joys of tabulation, the ardour of research, and the
feverish delights of historical controversy, that
they seem to forget that although history is about
dead men, they were not always dead.

But, I imagine, most of us are agreed that the
historian's business is to bring them to life again ;
and that is nowhere harder than in the case of
Palmerston.   May I say why ?   There seem to me
to be two main obstacles to a proper knowledge of
Lord Palmerston.   The first is this :   I believe
there is no statesman of the nineteenth century
of whom there is a more rigid or a more universal
stock portrait than there is of Palmerston.   Open
any book that you like, turn to the references to
Lord Palmerston, and you will invariably find the
same lay figure in the same attitude described in
the same *cliché*.   You all know the formula—a
free use of the adjective "jaunty", an almost
equally frequent application of the adjective
"flippant", sometimes varied by the use of the
adjective "truculent", helped out by a couple of
slightly indecorous anecdotes and a reference to
the fact that *Punch* used to draw him with a
straw in his mouth,—a circumstance which once
so far misled a literal-minded foreign historian
that you will find in Treitschke's *History of Germany*

in the Nineteenth Century, somewhere in the fifth
volume, a description of Lord Palmerston walking
up Parliament Street after the rising of the House
with his hat on the back of his head and " a
flower always in his mouth or in his button-hole ",
looking, it would appear, like a cross between
a successful bookmaker and Carmen. That is an
extreme instance of the accepted caricature. But
in its normal form you will find the *cliché*—jaunty,
flippant, truculent—in almost any book that you
care to open on the nineteenth century from the
highest to the lowest.

I do not complain when one finds *clichés* in
text-books. Where do you expect to find a
cliché, if not in a text-book ? After all, one
could never pass examinations without *clichés*.
But it is a serious thing when a caricature of
this class pervades the higher type of historical
literature, as it has in this case ; and it is, to my
mind, a serious obstacle to knowledge. It is stupid,
because when you ask how this elderly imbecile,
with the manners of a stable-boy, and no notion
in his head beyond a promiscuous desire to insult
foreigners, managed to be the leading figure in
Europe for thirty-five years, to be the successful
rival of Metternich, and the idol of his country for
the sufficient reason that he carried its name
higher than it has stood before or since, there is
no answer. If I may suggest one, it is that there

is something wrong with the accepted portrait of
Palmerston.

That is one obstacle to knowledge. May I
suggest a second ? It is that his career is custom-
arily studied from the wrong end. Like most of
us, he began at the beginning ; but so much that
has been written about him seems to begin from
the end. Indeed, so much of history has been
written backwards, in the mood of that figure of
chivalry in the bad historical play quoted or, as
I suspect, fabricated in one of M. Maurois' novels,
who is made to say in addressing his army, " Let
us remember, we men of the Middle Ages, that
to-morrow we start for the Hundred Years' War ".
That somewhat misleading mood of wisdom after
the event is the mood in which a great deal of
history has been written ; and I would say to you
this afternoon that it is hardly a mood in which
you can hope to reconstruct with any accuracy a
man's growth or a man's reality. It may account
for the attempt that is almost invariably made to
study the Palmerston of 1830 or 1840 by the light
—the rather failing and uncertain light—of the
Palmerston of 1865.

It appears to be almost universally assumed that
because Palmerston died at the age of eighty, he
was born at the age of eighty. Statesmen have an
odd way of fastening themselves in the popular
imagination at particular ages. I suppose that there

was no passage in Mr. Wells' *Outline of History* that caused more alarm than that in which he described Mr. Gladstone as " a white-faced, black-haired man of incredible energy ". Now, you will never grasp Mr. Gladstone, if you study him in the light of the " Grand Old Man " ; and you will miss the greater part of Lord Palmerston, if you regard him solely as " Old Pam ". It is easy enough to erect the usual lay figure at an advanced age and to propel it, with appropriate comments, through the various stages of Lord Palmerston's career. But that method leaves so many questions unanswered. Why did this man, having been a Tory, become a Whig ? How did he suddenly leap into something like European domination ? Those are two questions which are left utterly unanswered by the " Old Pam " formula ; and you will forgive me if I prefer a less simple method.

II

Our knowledge of Palmerston is curiously truncated. You will have noticed, in the case of another statesman, how the lives of Wellington nearly all stop with an almost audible click after the battle of Waterloo, adding in a hasty undertone that he survived until 1852 and was Prime Minister from time to time. The exact opposite has been the case with our knowledge of Palmerston.

We know all about his later years. From the moment that he goes to the Foreign Office in 1830, he moves in the broad daylight of history. But before 1830 he is as obscure a figure as Lord Goderich or Mr. Spencer Perceval, and that is dim enough. It is almost as though he were shot up through a trap-door at the age of forty-six to go to the Foreign Office and take charge of British policy in 1830. I may have slightly overstated it, because we are actually told that he had been Secretary at War for a great many years, that he rarely spoke in debate, and that he was much seen at Almack's under the attractive nickname of " Cupid ". And we are asked to accept without surprise the sudden emergence of this unimpressive blend of a conscientious official with an excellent dancer as the leading statesman in Europe at a time when it still contained Metternich and Talleyrand. I suggest to you that some explanation of this singular event is to be found in those first forty-five years of his career, which have been so strangely ignored —the more so if you are concerned to ascertain his political principles. I do not know whether our Chairman would agree with me that it is always easier to find a man's principles at the beginning of his career than at the end, because in the later stages principles are so lamentably apt to become obscured by practice. It was the practice of Napoleon to have a definite plan for the opening movement in a campaign and then to proceed according to circumstances. I am afraid that is an attitude to which men are often forced in politics. So you will find far more of their actual design in their early than in their later years. For that reason I would direct your attention to Lord Palmerston's beginnings.

III

The first suggestion that I would make is founded on a simple fact of chronology, undisputed even by the highest authorities. Lord Palmerston, who died in 1865, was born in 1784. His career is an amazing bridge between the eighteenth and the nineteenth centuries. He was born in the year in which Reynolds painted *The Tragic Muse*, and died in the year after Mr. Swinburne published *Atalanta in Calydon*. I have often seen him described as typical of mid-Victorian complacency. To me he has seemed rather to be the last fragment of the eighteenth century projecting far into the nineteenth. He was the last of the Regency bucks— and the Regency was the last flicker of the eighteenth century. He was the last of the Canningites— and Mr. Canning was the last of the Pittites. I think we must never forget that Lord Palmerston spent the first sixteen years of his life in the eighteenth century. And that was not a mere accident of chronology ; it was not a mere coincidence. His life, if one studies his parents, was rooted right in the heart of the eighteenth century. You will find his father in Horace Walpole and Boswell and Fanny Burney; and he wrote verse at Bath—the sort of verse that a Viscount would write at Bath. An ode on his first marriage was composed by a young officer of cavalry who afterwards became General Burgoyne and surrendered at Saratoga. Lord Palmerston's father was a close friend of Sir Joshua Reynolds. He was blackballed for the Club just before Palmerston was born. After the boy's birth in 1784 the family lived in a smart Whig set, where Charles Fox and Sheridan dined, and Mrs. Sheridan sang for them, and some one said it was all " very junkety " in their house in Queen Anne's Gate, or at Sheen, or at Broadlands, which is still the eighteenth century itself.

Palmerston has always seemed to me to retain an eighteenth-century quality from his boyhood. If you ask me to define that quality, I would say that it consists of precisely those things which shocked nineteenth-century observers; of those easy manners which first led the originator of the *cliché* to call him " jaunty " ; of that light touch which made them call him " flippant ". Do you remember the drawing in which a caricaturist of genius in our own time, desiring to portray

I

"the grave misgivings of the nineteenth century, and the wicked amusement of the eighteenth, in watching the progress (or whatever it is) of the twentieth", represents two figures standing to watch our own century, one of whom takes snuff and the other quite obviously reads Herbert Spencer? That contrast has always seemed to me to explain the levity of Lord Palmerston, which so shocked his younger contemporaries. And, above all, there is the positive quality of his mind. Palmerston and the eighteenth century were never in doubt: the nineteenth century was always in doubt. Palmerston and the eighteenth century never asked questions: they answered them.

But, as it seems to me, there is much more than a mere general quality that he derives from the century of his origin. It also made a quite definite contribution to his education and training. If I may say so with all possible respect within these walls, when one is studying the influences upon any man, it is far less important to ascertain where he spent his terms than where he spent his vacations; and in the case of Palmerston it seems to me a fact of the utmost significance that a considerable amount of time in his earlier years—his undergraduate and immediately post-graduate years—was spent in the society of Lord Malmesbury. His influence on Palmerston is undoubted. Lord Palmerston's father died in 1801, and Malmesbury became his guardian. The youth was a regular visitor at Park Place. When Palmerston finished his education, it was Lord Malmesbury who approached the Prime Minister and got him his first post, a minor place in the Admiralty. When Mr. Spencer Perceval invited a boy of twenty-five to be Chancellor of the Exchequer and he refused, Palmerston had consulted Malmesbury throughout as to whether he should accept the appointment.

What was his influence likely to be ? So far as home politics were concerned, I think that Malmesbury had a great deal to do with determining Palmerston's definite desertion of the Whig tradition of his family and his acceptance of the position of a Pittite. For Malmesbury was one of those Whigs who were scared into patriotism and loyalty to Mr. Pitt by their country's danger.

But his great influence on Palmerston lay in his view of Europe. Malmesbury had been a diplomat at the Courts of Frederick the Great and Catherine the Great, and he was now the oracle of Mr. Pitt and the official world upon foreign affairs. I suggest that it is a matter of the utmost importance that Lord Palmerston learned his Europe from an " old master " of the eighteenth century. That is a training from which a man might well emerge with a belief that the normal state of Europe, to which it was trying to struggle

back to after the War—people always imagine
that they can get back to normal after a war—
was the diplomatic anarchy which had marked the
last years of the European monarchies before the
Revolution. He would emerge with a belief that
we could change our allies, as allies had been
changed in the eighteenth century, like partners
in a dance ; that there were no such things as
immutable principles of European policy or all
the impressive apparatus created by the Vienna
treaties and the Holy Alliance. A man trained
in the eighteenth century might well think of the
Holy Alliance and the doctrines of Metternich
as an unnatural restraint on free rotation from
one ally to the other ; that *les peuples n'ont pas
des cousins* ; that, as Lord Palmerston said in
his Polish speech in 1848, " It is a narrow policy
to suppose that this country or that is to be
marked as the eternal ally or the perpetual
enemy of England. We have no eternal allies and
we have no perpetual enemies. Our interests are
eternal and perpetual." A man would emerge from
such a training with a conviction that Metternich
was mostly wrong ; and I have sometimes wondered
whether Lord Palmerston's attitude to the Austrian
system of reaction, which makes him appear one
of the sponsors of the nineteenth century, was
not due in its origins to an effort—perhaps un-
conscious—to reach back into the eighteenth

century rather than forward into the nineteenth
century.

IV

Now let me say something of another line of
influence upon his formation. His formal education, conducted with becoming pomp at Harrow
and Cambridge, was of the type that lends dignity
to a man's obituary without unduly modifying his
attainments. But his training contained other and
less hallowed elements. There was a good deal of
the foreign tutor and of foreign travel. One finds
him travelling abroad at a particularly early age ;
and that left memories which remained. At nine he
was in Italy with his father, and in Switzerland
and Bavaria with an Italian master. One finds him
at ten writing letters in French and Italian. His
French—I blush to say it of a Foreign Secretary—
remained perfect through life. You will find him
as a serious traveller on the Continent in 1815 and
1818. He was abroad just after Waterloo, investi-
gating every point of interest in countless roadside
conversations. He made a second visit at the end
of the Allied occupation in 1818. When he at last
got out of office in 1828, almost for the first time
after leaving the nursery, you find him in Paris
and again in 1829, having the dreariest conversations on public affairs with the statesmen
who were steering Charles X. straight into the

Revolution of 1830. You will find in his letters home and diaries a perfectly serious investigation of the state of affairs in foreign countries—a singular contrast to the half-witted John Bull of Palmerstonian legend, who is supposed to spend the greater part of his life making enemies of foreigners.

Then comes an influx of Liberal ideas. One phase of his education was conducted in Edinburgh at the residence of Professor Dugald Stewart, a pupil of Adam Smith. You will find Palmerston attending his lectures and taking copious notes—a circumstance from which you will not, I hope, infer that he did not understand what was being said. It was an education in a sound disbelief in restraints on trade, an admirable preparation for the advent of Huskisson and the Anti-Corn Law League.

Another strain of influence comes from his position as an Irish landlord. It is unusual for such a position to be considered an apprenticeship in Liberalism ; but Palmerston's history in that respect is very remarkable. You will find him visiting his Irish estates in 1808, full of generous plans not only for the wise economic development of the property, but for the introduction of schools and teachers, who, he says boldly, will probably have to be Catholics. In 1812 he gave a vote for Catholic Emancipation, although he was an Under-Secretary in what was probably the most Tory Government this country has ever seen.   In 1813, when Catholic Emancipation made its annual appearance in the House of Commons, he spoke on it, although he rarely spoke on anything except his purely departmental War Office business.   He began by arguing that the Catholics cannot possibly have any rights, because otherwise Parliament could not be bargaining with them ; for, as Parliament cannot err, it follows that they cannot have any rights.   The peculiar reasoning was manifestly self-taught.   From that he proceeds to an extraordinarily bold argument on the simple footing of expediency.   How far is it expedient that you should cut off from the public service an entire section of the population ? And he speculates what would have happened " if by the circumstances of birth and education a Nelson, a Wellington, a Burke, a Fox or a Pitt, had belonged to this class ".   He went on voting steadily for Catholic Emancipation against the majority of his Tory colleagues.   In 1825, when he was member for the University of Cambridge, his University petitioned, with the gusto which you would expect of a University in 1825, against Catholic Emancipation ; and Palmerston presented the petition in absolute silence.   In 1826 he fought an election and nearly lost it by reason of his Catholic sympathies, an election which did a great deal to determine his drift from Toryism to

Whiggery. In 1827 he did a most striking thing, making a concordat with his Roman Catholic Bishop and so getting the children on his estate into his schools. In 1826 he, though an Irish landlord, wrote .

The days of Protestant ascendancy I think are numbered. It is strange that in this enlightened age and civilised country people should be still debating whether it is wise to convert four or five millions of men from enemies to friends and whether it is *safe* to give peace to Ireland.

Now, in the mouth of Burke or Gladstone that would be hailed as a splendid gleam of his passion for freedom. In an obscure letter of Lord Palmerston's it is unnoticed. I suggest to you that it is part of the explanation of how the Tory placeman of twenty years turned Whig; and it was a vital part of his preparation to receive the influence of Mr. Canning, as well as for that rather stormy Cambridge election in 1826, from which he emerged part Whig and no part Tory.

V

I must say something of the final element in his training, the fact that he spent nineteen years at the War Office. In 1809 he refused the Chancellorship of the Exchequer, preferring to be Secretary at War, because, as he said, the office was "better suited to a beginner". The War Depart-

ment was at the moment at war with Napoleon.
He spent six years at the War Office in time of
war, and thirteen years more in time of peace ;
and in those neglected years, which lie buried
under the cairns of the Record Office, I think
you will find some of the most vital ingredients
which make up the familiar figure of Lord
Palmerston. We are always told that he was
pre-eminently English. I know of no sounder
school of patriotism than the War Office. One
is bound to confess that there were occasions
in his dealings with foreign powers when he was
admittedly peremptory ; though he was rarely
peremptory when it was not safe. It is only mild-
mannered ministers who make wars. But there
was sometimes a certain sharpness in Lord Palmerston's tone. Never forget that he got his first
six years of official training at the War Office during
a European war. That is a training from which a
man might easily emerge with a belief that a frigate
and a battalion of the line were the normal mes-
sengers of British policy.

And there is another side to it. Palmerston
was a master of paper work, and there could be
no better school of administration than nineteen
years of War Office drafting. Much of administration consists in disposing gracefully of grievances ;
and I am sure our Chairman, as an ex-Financial
Secretary to the War Office, will agree with me

that no richer field of grievances can be found than the War Department. Palmerston was responsible to Parliament and the civil authorities for the conduct of soldiers, and I have often thought that those nineteen years taught him something of his amazing loyalty to subordinates. But I think there is another element of the full-grown Palmerston that one can discern in the War Office years, his cheerful contentiousness. The War Office was a promising field for administrative debate. The War Office was at war with Napoleon; but branches of the War Office were even more profoundly at war with one another.

Now let me tell you one story of a War Office dispute in Lord Palmerston's time, which may give you some idea of the school from which he emerged. The army was governed by a Secretary of State for War and the Colonies, a Secretary at War (which was Palmerston's position), and a Commander-in-Chief. The dispute, which was not unduly abbreviated, lasted for thirteen years. It related to the happy and fruitful theme of Army clothing. Army clothing resided in a sort of administrative " No Man's Land ", or devastated area, between the War Department and the military. In 1810 the Secretary at War introduced, with somewhat unworthy stealth, a Bill to transfer control from the military to his own department. The House of Commons was looking, as it generally

does, the other way; and the Bill passed. The
Commander-in-Chief in 1810 was Sir David
Dundas, one of Chatham's young men, who, being
still alive, was made Commander-in-Chief against
Napoleon. Sir David Dundas took it, on the whole,
very well. He made no violent protest to his
young colleague; but he appealed, with the weary
gesture of a nurse appealing to the parent of a
fractious child, to the Prime Minister. The Prime
Minister determined the administrative border-line
between the two departments. But at this moment
one begins to see a glimpse of the true Palmerston.
For at that very moment the rash young man
committed the almost nameless crime of calling
upon the Army for a duplicate of a monthly return
of bread and forage, and even threatened to alter
the form of pay-warrant in force for Generals.
There was a prompt explosion. The cheerful young
Secretary at War wrote to the Prime Minister that
his elderly colleague was " a little irritable and
hasty in transacting business, and apt to take up a
matter before he is quite in possession of all the
facts of the case ". There was an appeal to the
Prince Regent; and that august creature settled
the dispute under the Sign Manual itself. Then
there was a change of Commander-in-Chief; the
Duke of York returned to office; and within a
very few months Palmerston was at it again in a
terrific memorandum, that you may read in the

first volume of his *Life*, in which he argued with
copious precedents the precise limits of departmental authority since the days of Queen Anne.
A Cabinet committee sat ; Lord Eldon, the Chancellor, wrote opinions on the legal aspect of the case.
The papers were sent to Sir David Dundas, who
was now in retirement at Chelsea Hospital and
enlivened his leisure by decorating them with
offensive *marginalia* containing the most sulphurous
comments. The war went on. In 1814, as
Napoleon fell back across France, some one wrote
that the dispute was "drawing to a close ".
1815—Waterloo—St. Helena—1821—the Emperor
dies—and still, in 1823 and a world at peace,
there were faint echoes of the debate. That is the
school of administration in which Lord Palmerston
learned his touch.

VI

Let me now mention, very briefly, two further
influences upon his formation. First, Mr. Canning.
There were two elements in Mr. Canning that were
bound to attract Palmerston : his attitude to the
Roman Catholic question and, even more than that,
his attitude to Europe. The choice before any
young man in the early and middle 'twenties was
between the " European " attitude of Lord Castlereagh, whose reputation owes almost more to the
work of Professor C. K. Webster than to his own,

and the attitude of Mr. Canning, which he himself summarised as " For *Europe* I shall be desirous *now and then* to read *England* ". You cannot doubt which of those two attitudes was the more likely to attract Palmerston. It is an influence which, to my mind, was largely responsible for directing Palmerston to the topic of foreign affairs as the best field for applying the principles of Mr. Canning after his death. It is an influence which you will find in his treatment of half a dozen specific problems ; and it is always interesting to examine how far in his handling of them he was merely executing the codicils to the will of Mr. Canning.

It is an influence which you will even trace in his style as a public speaker. In 1829 he made two great speeches, from which he emerged as a man of note—one on the Catholic question, and the other on European policy. He clearly intended them to be his manifesto ; and one can fix his estimate of their importance by the fact that he himself had copies printed for distribution. You will find there a conscious and not unsuccessful imitation of Mr. Canning, adorned by one of his favourite similes. For as some statesmen are attracted by the possibilities of Welsh hills or English fields, Lord Palmerston and Mr. Canning reveal a common liking for the British line-of-battleship.

But, above all, you will find the influence
of Canning in the broad ideal of foreign policy,
which Canning himself stated in the most Palmerstonian style, that England might be " a model,
and ultimately perhaps an umpire ". That is the
formula, if you wish to find a short formula, of
Lord Palmerston's foreign policy.

VII

And the last influence was that of Princess Lieven,
whose society Palmerston owed to his great friendship with her friend Lady Cowper, and to his fre-
quentation of Almack's, where she reigned supreme.
In the early years, before he went to the Foreign
Office, you will always find him at the Lievens'.
One may imagine that the Princess coached him
in diplomacy as a useful mouthpiece of Russian
views. One even finds her pressing Lord Grey to
put him at the Foreign Office in 1830. He quite
thoughtlessly forgot the lessons that she taught
him about Russia. But there is one thing that
she must as a Russian have taught him and he
did not forget—to mistrust Austria and Metternich.
But that particular teaching of Princess Lieven
coincides with his eighteenth-century feeling that
Metternich was mostly wrong.

So it was not quite with a blank sheet he went

to the Foreign Office in 1830. You will find strands
of early influence wound into the skein of his later
career. The Canningite erected England as a
model in the eyes of Europe. The War Office man
continued for thirty-five years to conduct contro-
versies with the cheerful gusto with which he once
informed the Military Secretary officially that
" the War will be carried on with as much courtesy
as a State of Contest in its nature admits." And
the man of the eighteenth century recurs at every
turn—in his whole air, in his dress, for he belonged
to an age when a man could dress. Of what
other statesman could an ecstatic deputation
write that he was "dressed like a youth of
eighteen "? You will find it in his unhappy mis-
understanding of his sovereign. How could the
eighteenth century understand that embodiment
of the nineteenth? You will find it in his attitude
to the United States. You cannot expect any
undue awe of revolted colonies in a statesman
born only two years after they were detached
from the Crown. You will find it in his brief
tenure of the Home Office, in his extraordinarily
bold reforms. He was one of the most reforming
of Home Secretaries, for the simple reason that the
eighteenth century had no particular respect for the
mushroom magnates of the Industrial Revolution.
And you will find it at the very end, when the
old man was dying. An obtrusive doctor came to

his bedside and, oppressed by the fact that it was Sunday, could find nothing better to do than to pelt his patient with a hail of rather Evangelical questions as to the state of his religious beliefs. His answer to the interrogation, which was both eloquent and prolonged, gave entire satisfaction to the doctor, and consisted of the one word, " Certainly ". That answer, with its perfect courtesy in face of the ill-timed ardour of 1865 at its most improving, has always seemed the last word of the eighteenth century.

EARL RUSSELL, K.G.

From the painting by Sir F. Grant, in the National Portrait Gallery

LORD JOHN RUSSELL

By W. F. REDDAWAY

I

RUSSELL was born in 1792, when Europe was taking up arms to put down the French Revolution. He died in 1878, when the statesmen were assembling at Berlin to defend the authority of Europe over the Eastern question. He had been a member of the Legislature for sixty-five years, nearly fifty in the Commons. For half a century he ranked as the protagonist of Reform. During thirty-seven years he stood first or second in the Liberal party, and for nearly four-fifths of that period his party was substantially in power. For some six years, comprising the climax of British and European trouble about 1848, he was Prime Minister. For forty years at least he was always a considerable factor in Britain; usually, in Europe; and not seldom, in the world. To learn by what means and on what principles he won and wielded power is therefore indispensable to a knowledge of the nineteenth century.

K

The authorities for a full biography of Russell are innumerable. Concealment he neither needed nor practised nor desired. He has himself bequeathed a fragmentary autobiography, two volumes of selected speeches and despatches, and several treatises on history. His official biography is the accurate work of Spencer Walpole : it is supplemented by the authoritative short biography of Reid and by a full and well-documented memoir of his second wife : two volumes of his early correspondence have been edited by his son : two volumes of the later, quite recently, by Dr. Gooch. The immensity of Hansard, the Public Records, and the contemporary press lies behind. The ordinary student finds himself confronted by that rampart of biographies and diaries—none of them readily dispensable, though many too decent for perfect truth—which acts like a tariff wall in safeguarding British historical industry against foreign competition. Dr. Gooch mentions twenty-nine recent biographical or autobiographical works of this kind.

The student who comforts his conscience with the thought that he has only one lifetime to dispose of, and that digestion must count for something, finds himself further challenged by the diversity of judgment among his most trusted friends. Of four eminent historians who have lately pronounced on Russell, one speaks of his " unimaginative apathy " at a crisis ; another terms him an " artist in abuse, lecturing the whole world with colossal impudence "; a third thinks it necessary to cite the Reform Bill and Italian unity to palliate a general charge of failure ; a fourth declares that " his share in the making of modern England is equalled by Lord Grey alone ".

Such indications perhaps point merely to the fact that our material is too copious and our perspective as yet too short to warrant a final judgment. In an age of Bolshevists and Fascisti " a Russell, sweet Liberty's champion ", commands no automatic allegiance. But Russell, whom his friends described as entirely unlike anybody else, has always evoked a diversity of estimate greater even than that which falls to the lot of almost every statesman. To Shaftesbury he was " a political intriguer and the unfeeling adversary of the wretched chimney-sweeps ". Disraeli once defined his birthright as feeble intellect and strong ambition. Walpole, surveying his whole career, can claim that the vast material progress of Britain from the 'twenties to the 'sixties was equalled by her progress in law and morals, and that in this he took a leading share.

II

The criticism of a class of Honoursmen was once invited on three diverse estimates of his work and worth. The first was taken from the unmeasured invective of Carlyle and written in 1850 when Russell was first Prime Minister. " I, then," the Premier is supposed to say on finding himself the governor of England, " I, then, am the ablest of English attainable men. . . . The best-combined sample of whatsoever divine qualities are in this big people, the consummate flower of all that they have done and been, the ultimate product of the destinies and English man of men, arrived at last in the fullness of time, is—who think you ? Ye worlds, the Ithuriel javelin by which, with all these accumulated energies old and new, the English People means to smite and pierce, is this poor tailor's-bodkin, hardly adequate to bore an eyelet-hole." The second estimate came from a modern German essay, whose author styled Russell " undoubtedly honourable and well-meaning, but no statesman ", and declared that " poverty of ideas stamps him as a dilettante in his books and his politics alike ". The third was Lord Houghton's tribute : " the highest and most complete states-man of my generation ".

Confronted with these three, one candidate shrewdly observed that Russell " was no fool, and no genius—*except in letter-writing* ".

Letter-writing, indeed, was Russell's natural and favourite mode of self-expression. Though his " cool small voice " often uttered trenchant and effective speeches, "eloquence", he said, "I had none." From childhood, on the other hand, he was a ready writer. Unusual restlessness in him might be diagnosed as "suppressed epistle".

More often nature had its way, and his clear thought passed by the post to a single person or to the world with that dry directness which was all his own. "My dear Melbourne", he wrote to the Prime Minister in 1835, "I am afraid you do not take exercise enough or eat and drink more than enough. One of the two may do, but not both together." Written with equal point and plainness, the Edinburgh Letter, the Durham Letter, the despatch on the Italian question, which was regarded as worth more than 100,000 men—these are leading events in the history of the time. The letter to the bishops who had protested against the appointment of Dr. Hampden to the See of Hereford contains so much of Russell that I should cite it in full were it not easily accessible in Walpole. Of no less biographical and historical value is his despatch on the Cuban question, written seventy-three years ago, on February 16, 1853. France and Britain had proposed to the United States a triple self-denying ordinance regarding Cuba, then in chronic rebellion against Spain. The United States, with their normal suspicion of the old-world diplomacy and with flexible notions of the so-called "doctrine" of Monroe, had replied at great length in a sense which Russell's language will make clear. The despatch, I think, well illustrates his ruthless logic, his frank delight in a debating " score ", his unconsciousness that a plain statement of the truth may give offence, and his jealousy for the rights of Britain. Its composition, together with the conference with the French ambassador, must have occupied the chief of a day that might perhaps have been more profitably devoted to studying the designs of Russia, then intent on the advance which was foiled by the Crimean War.

" It is doubtless ", Russell admits, " perfectly within the competence of the American Government to reject the proposal that was made by Lord Malmesbury and M. Turgot in reference to Cuba. Each Government will then remain as free as it was before to take that course which its sense of duty, and regard for the interests of its people, may prescribe.

" I should have satisfied my obligations as Secretary of State by this obvious remark, had not Mr. Everett entered at large into arguments which the simple nature of the question before him hardly seemed to require.

" The Governments of Great Britain and France, when they made this proposal to that of the United States, were fully aware of the growth of power and extension of territory which have marked the progress of the United States since the period of their independence.

" The absorption or annexation of Louisiana in 1803, of Florida in 1819, of Texas in 1845, and of California in 1848 had not escaped them. Still less did they require to be reminded of the events of the Seven Years' War or of the American War. It occurs to Her Majesty's Govern-

ment therefore to ask *for what purpose* are these arguments
introduced with so much preparation, and urged with so
much ability ? It would appear that the purpose, not
fully avowed, but hardly concealed, is to procure the
admission of a doctrine that the United States have an
interest in Cuba to which Great Britain and France cannot
pretend. In order to meet this pretension it is necessary
to set forth the character of the two Powers who made the
offer in question. Mr. Everett declares in the outset of
his despatch that ' The United States would not see with
indifference the Island of Cuba fall into the possession of
any other European Government than Spain, etc.' The
two Powers most likely to possess themselves of Cuba,
and most formidable to the United States, are Great Britain
and France. Great Britain is in possession, by treaty, of
the Island of Trinidad, which, in the last century, was a
colony of Spain : France was in possession, at the com-
mencement of this century, of Louisiana, by voluntary
cession from Spain. These two Powers, by their naval
resources, are in fact the only Powers who could be rivals
with the United States for the possession of Cuba. Well !
these two Powers are ready voluntarily to ' declare,
severally and collectively, that they will not obtain for
themselves, or for any one of themselves, any exclusive
control over the said Island ' (of Cuba) ' nor assume nor
exercise any dominion over the same '. Thus if the object
of the United States was to bar the acquisition of Cuba
by any European state, this convention would secure that
object.

" But if it is intended on the part of the United States
to maintain that Great Britain and France have no interest
in the maintenance of the present *status quo* in Cuba ; and
that the United States have alone a right to a voice in
that matter, Her Majesty's Government at once refuse to
admit such a claim. Her Majesty's possessions in the
West Indies alone, without insisting on the importance to

Mexico and other friendly states of the present distribution of power, give Her Majesty an interest in this question which she cannot forgo. The possessions of France in the American Seas give a similar interest to France which, no doubt, will be put forward by her Government.

" Nor is this right at all invalidated by the argument of Mr. Everett that Cuba is to the United States as an island at the mouth of the Thames or the Seine would be to England or France. The distance of Cuba from the nearest part of the territory of the United States, namely, from the southernmost point of Florida, is one hundred and ten miles. An island at an equal distance from the mouth of the Thames would be placed about ten miles north of Antwerp in Belgium. An island at the same distance from Jamaica would be placed at Manzanilla, a town in Cuba. Thus there are no grounds for saying that the possession of Cuba by Great Britain or France would be menacing to the United States, but its possession by the United States would not be so to Great Britain. There is one argument of the Secretary of State which appears to Her Majesty's Government not only unfounded but disquieting. Lord Malmesbury and M. de Turgot put forward as a reason for entering into the proposed compact, ' the attacks which have lately been made on the Island of Cuba by lawless bands of adventurers from the United States, and with the avowed design of taking possession of that island '. To this reason Mr. Everett replies in these terms : ' The President is convinced that the conclusion of such a treaty, instead of putting a stop to these lawless proceedings, would give a new and powerful impulse to them.' The Government of Great Britain acknowledges with respect the conduct of the President in disavowing and discouraging the lawless attempts here referred to. The character of those attempts indeed was such as to excite the reprobation of every civilised State. The spectacle of bands of men collected together, in reckless disregard of treaties, for the purpose of making from the ports of the United States a piratical attack on the territory of a power in amity with their own State, and, when there, endeavouring by armed invasion to excite the obedient to revolt and the tranquil to disturbance, was a sight shocking, no doubt, to the just and honest principles of the President. But the statement made by the President that a convention, duly signed and legally ratified, engaging to respect the present state of possession in all future time, would but excite these bands of pirates to more violent breaches of all the laws of honesty and good neighbourhood, is a melancholy avowal for the Chief of a great State. Without disputing its truth, Her Majesty's Government may express a hope that this state of things will not endure ; and that the citizens of the United States, while they justly boast of their institutions, will not be insensible to the value of those eternal laws of right and wrong, of peace and friendship, and of duty to our neighbours, which ought to guide every Christian nation. Nor can a people so enlightened fail to perceive the utility of those rules for the observance of international relations which for centuries have been known to Europe by the name of the Law of Nations. Among the commentators on that law some of the most distinguished American citizens have earned an enviable reputation ; and it is difficult to suppose that the United States would set the example of abrogating its most sacred provisions. Nor let it be said that such a convention would have prevented the inhabitants of Cuba from asserting their independence. With regard to internal troubles the proposed convention was altogether silent. But a pretended declaration of independence, with a view of immediately seeking refuge from revolts on the part of the Blacks under the shelter of the United States, would justly be looked upon as the same, in effect, as a formal annexation.

" Finally, while fully admitting the right of the United

States to reject the proposal made by Lord Malmesbury and M. de Turgot, Great Britain must at once resume her entire liberty, and, upon any occasion that may call for it, be free to act, either singly or in conjunction with other powers, as to her may seem fit."

Nine years later, Russell declared that "the Yankee Government" had "all the genius of a country attorney".

"No people", wrote Palmerston in 1844, "not even excepting the Irish peasantry, look more keenly into the minds of those they have to deal with, to discover anything like wavering or infirmity of purpose, or know better how to take advantage of it". They would seek it in vain in a despatch which, like the letter to the Bishops, redolent of the eighteenth century in which France gave point and edge to the steel of English prose, appears, and was, unanswerable save by the human expedient of continuing to disagree. And it is characteristic of Russell that he habitually ignored or underrated the human weakness of mankind. Himself endowed, as an opponent admitted, with "a judgment clear, prompt and undisturbed by passion" and "a will which is inflexible", in home and in foreign affairs alike he would proclaim the truth as he saw it, and bear the illogical but natural consequences with an equanimity which his colleagues did not always share. Remonstrating in 1852 with one who had said that Russell, if excluded, would "break everything to pieces like a bull in a china shop ", he points with well-founded gratification to the fact that " amongst all the charges brought against me this one of dishonesty has never found any credit ".

III

Russell was a great letter-writer, but was he a great man ? That is the question which will guide such investigation of his principles and of his career as is possible to me to-day. First of all, since in forty years his memory must in some degree have faded, let us strive to regain " some ocular view or imagination " of Russell " as a fact among facts ". That which first impressed every one who met him was his small size. The solid squires of the unreformed House of Commons could not understand how a little fellow weighing scarcely eight stone could propose to suppress their seats. Disraeli compared him to an Egyptian sacred beetle. Sydney Smith, who wrote to him, " I will fight you to the last drop of my ink and dine with you to the last drop of your claret ", told the mob, who were disappointed at the small-ness of their champion, that he had formerly been much larger, but was reduced through his anxiety on account of them. "Lord John", wrote Miss Eden when he was nearing seventy, " has shot a wild boar. Just conceive the indignation of the wild boar, if he had a moment's consciousness before death, to see the very small *human* who had murdered him." W. E. Forster, himself a giant, wrote after their first encounter, " What a strange little mortal he is to be ruler of a mighty nation, with his dwarf-like form and long, deep, remarkable head, and icy cold expression, with every now and then a look of fire ! "

No one who knows democracy can question the importance of the ideas formed by the people of statesmen or living men. That Russell could be portrayed as a bantam, or a boy chalking up " No Popery " and running away, that he could be thought of generally as " Johnny ", were factors in determining victory or defeat at the polls and affecting the assignment of office. A languid air and superficial coldness distinguished him throughout his life, chilling the party to which he was devoted and accentuating the differences betweeen its social elements. Forster's words, " He received me very cordially—for him " in 1866 may stand for a thousand instances. Clarendon did not appreciate being invited to go as Lord-Lieutenant to Ireland " in his most cold, short, abrupt, indifferent manner ; much as if he was disposing of a tide-waiter's place to an applicant ".

That in his family circle Russell proved himself generous, tender, simple, cheerful, even playful, could not abolish the general impression of him as the embodiment of chilling pride. How then could such a man become one of the two or three who alone could govern the House of Commons, then an undisciplined assembly of gentlemen who had little to fear from their constituents, and who were jealous above all things of their independence and personal honour ? Mainly, I think, in virtue of his other most salient characteristics, self-possession, pluck, sincerity, and power of mind. Though he protested against Sydney Smith's famous caricature, it holds too much of the truth to be omitted.

Lord John Russell . . . is ignorant of all moral fear ; there is nothing he would not undertake. I believe he would perform the operation for the stone, build St. Peter's, or assume (with or without ten minutes' notice) the command of the Channel Fleet ; and no one would discover by his manner that the patient had died, the church tumbled down, and the Channel Fleet been knocked to atoms.

Early in his career in Parliament he kept the House waiting for half an hour and began his speech quite unembarrassed. He could jest with Queen Victoria about her title to the throne of England. John Bright records a characteristic view of " the little man jogging along on his pony and looking as well satisfied with himself as if he were insulting the Catholics in the House of Commons "

Gladstone placed him for parliamentary courage by the side of Peel and of Disraeli, and his parlia-

mentary courage was never more splendid than
when he rose to protect a fellow-Whig or even a
Radical against unmerited attack. Outside the
walls of the House, too, he knew not fear. It was
by sheer manhood that he kept his seat for the
city in 1857, when his former agent declared that
he might as well expect to be made Pope, and
thought it possible his votes would number no
more than two or three.

For his country he was ready to make any
sacrifice, but he honestly believed that the sacrifice
that would most profit her was that of his own
freedom from the cares of office. Though he said
" Let us be Englishmen first and economists afterwards ", and confessed that he was no judge of
figures, he did not hesitate in 1848 himself to bring
in a budget. " In the country," said Disraeli, " a
menagerie before feeding-time could alone give an
idea of the unearthly yell with which it was
received ". The Government in that year per-
formed the unexampled feat of bringing in four
separate budgets.

Seven years later, in the thick of the Crimean
struggle, he broke up the Coalition Government by
a sudden resignation. This to his colleagues was
either treachery or panic, yet he calmly attempted
to include them in a new Government under
himself. And although in 1866 he had abdicated
and refused a seat in the Cabinet, in 1868, when

power came again to his party, he attempted to choose ministers and summon Liberals to his house as though he were still their head.

IV

Russell was born on 18th August 1792, two months before the natural time. This accident, it may safely be surmised, coloured the whole of his career. It made him a small and sickly youth, forced into egotism about his health, incapable of enduring a public school, and inevitably somewhat self-centred. Although careful living enabled him to survive almost to eighty-six, he had no reserve of vitality, and fell below his best at an earlier age than was natural for a statesman who lived so temperate a life. To this initial handicap may probably be ascribed what Lord Morley calls his " peculiar temperament—hard to agitate, but easy to nettle ". Gladstone, irritated into frankness, summed up his career in 1868 by writing to a fellow-sufferer :

A great reputation built itself up on the basis of splendid services for thirty years ; for almost twenty it has been, I fear, on the decline.

The cause may well have been that, in Gladstone's own later words,

With a slender store of physical power, his life was a daily assertion of the superiority of the spirit to the flesh.

It would not surprise me if in truth the slender store of physical power which he inherited formed the chief cause of most of the outstanding blemishes in Russell's long career.

" It was characteristic of my husband ", wrote his widow in perhaps the most valuable single passage available for his biography, " to bear patiently for a long while with difficulties, opposition, perplexities, doubts raised by those with whom he acted, listening to them with candour and good temper, and only meeting their arguments with his own, but at last, if he failed to convince them, to take a sudden resolution—either yielding to them entirely or breaking with them altogether—from which nothing could shake him, but which, on looking back in after years, did not always seem to him the best course. My father [Lord Minto], who knew him well, once said to me, half in jest and half in earnest : ' Your husband is never so determined as when he is in the wrong.' It was a relief to him to have done with hesitation and be resolved on any step which this very anxiety to have done with hesitation led him to believe a right one at the moment. This habit of mind showed itself in private as in public matters, and his children and I were often startled by abrupt decisions on home affairs announced very often by letter."

When he was nine years old, on 11th October 1801, his ailing mother died, a shock which could hardly fail to accentuate the sense of isolation of her devoted youngest son. Less than five months later, by the death of an uncle, he found himself Lord John Russell, son of the fifth Duke of Bedford, that is of a potentate who inherited immense estates and power. To the boy all avenues in the

great world were thenceforth open. The disciple
of Fox, almost the patron of Scott, he could command the best attentions of Wellington in the
Peninsula and of Napoleon at Elba. There he
found the fallen Emperor " very fat " and " very
gay ", " without much majesty in his air and still
less terror in his looks ", and learned from him
that Wellington was undoubtedly aiming at the
Crown. In 1813, while absent from England and
still lacking the legal qualification of full age, he
was loyally returned to Parliament by the Duke's
vassals of Tavistock. Thirteen years later, when
he had lost his seat at Huntingdon, he received a
kind note from another Duke : " I find that my
alternate nomination to the borough of Bandon is
still at my disposal. . . . I hope that you will
not be dissatisfied at finding yourself *elected* ".

Such an upbringing could hardly fail to increase
the already disproportionate attention to himself
that resulted from his early weakness. It also
emphasised his ingrained aristocracy. The name of
Russell, as Dr. Gooch has finely said, was in itself
a programme.

" In all times of popular movement ", wrote Lord John
to the Duke, his brother, in 1841, " the Russells have been
on the ' forward ' side. At the Reformation the first Earl
of Bedford ; in Charles I.'s days Francis the great Earl ; in
Charles II.'s William, Lord Russell ; in later times Francis
Duke of Bedford—my father—you—and lastly myself in
the Reform Bill."

L

But with the Whig self-dedication to public service
went an inbred conviction that public service and
its rewards were for the Whigs. Croker wrote
with brutal truth : " Lord John . . . contrives
to unite an aristocratical confidence in himself and
his connections with very democratic views for the
rest of mankind ".   In his last Cabinet, a generation
after the Reform Bill, Gladstone was the only
member who was not born to rule, and for the
Admiralty the Duke of Somerset was declared
indispensable.

And with regard to patronage, as one of his
biographers explained with delicious naïveté, " while
remembering his relatives he did not neglect his
friends ".   " As you have no place on the sea,
perhaps you would like to be Warden of the Cinque
Ports ", he wrote to Granville.[1] To substitute
competitive examination for ministerial appointment as the door to the Civil Service seemed to
him entirely wrong, and he opposed Gladstone's
abolition of the purchase of commissions in the
army. If we learn with proud surprise that he
offered to pay Scott's debts from the public funds ;
if his Chancellor of the Exchequer learned, with
more surprise than pride, that he had promised a
loan to Morocco without reference to the Cabinet
or to himself, we must remember that this most

---

[1] The wardenship, it should be remembered, was not a post of
profit.

pure and high-minded statesman was born in the eighteenth century to a great Whig house.

V

I have touched on the early isolation which Russell, by nature most affectionate, met with gay courage ; on the vast bounty of fortune to his house, which did not make him personally rich or independent ; and on some of the sources from which his political principles were derived. During the six and twenty years which passed between his birth and his acceptance of politics as his lifework, other special factors had helped to make him what he ever afterwards remained. Born at the outbreak of the revolutionary war, he had grown to manhood as the contemporary of his country's triumph over Napoleon. He therefore shared the proud confidence of such men as Palmerston and Canning in the might and destiny of Britain. The champion of liberty and of law, he had the point of honour for the nation no less than for himself. In 1839, when the French inquired how much of Australia we claimed, he answered immediately " the whole ". In 1858, when Louis Napoleon had been all but blown up by bombs from Birmingham, Russell expressed his " great pain " at the idea that " any minister who had a regard for national dignity " should contemplate altering the law of

England after the utterance of threats by France. In 1865, after two years' hard thinking, he declared that " England would be disgraced for ever " if, at the bidding of the United States, such questions as, Was Lord Russell diligent or negligent ? or Was Sir Roundell Palmer versed in the laws of England ? were left to the arbitration of any foreign power.

The aspect of the world that had imprinted itself upon his mind when it was most plastic was that of France as the menace to liberty and England as its saviour. Preparedness for war and counsel from England therefore seemed to him natural. " Taxes may have to be imposed," he wrote in 1838, " and danger to the Government incurred, rather than the navy be weak and dispersed." " I know something of the English people," he declared in 1853, " and I feel sure that they would fight to the stumps for the honour of England." But " the honour of England ", as he wrote to the Queen, " does not consist in defending every English officer or English subject, right or wrong, but in taking care that she does not infringe the rules of justice, and that they are not infringed against her ". We, like other nations, should be guided by " the grand rule of doing to others as we wish that they should do unto us ". At the same time he was determined that England should not " forget her precedence of teaching the nations how to live ", and it was his fate to rehearse the attitude appropriate to the eclipse of Napoleon at the moment of the dawn of Bismarck. The inevitable insularity which he derived from the time and place of his birth had been corrected by the broadening influence of travel. Besides long visits to the Continent in war and in peace he knew Ireland as the son of a Lord Lieutenant and Scotland as a student at Edinburgh. Thus he was prepared for the discovery that in the Parliament of the 'thirties " it was not properly borne in mind that as England is inhabited by Englishmen, and Scotland by Scotchmen, so Ireland is inhabited by Irishmen ". This statesmanlike dictum struck Gladstone ineffaceably and dominated politics fifty years after its author, as premature with justice for Ireland as with esteem for the Colonies, had then upset the coach.

The fact that Russell was a member of the Legislature for nearly sixty-five years, and at twenty-seven an important member of the House of Commons, may easily obscure the truth that his first love was for letters. Until his health became more stable, indeed, the late hours and the foul air of the Parliament House were impossible for him, whereas in later days he found the time long until Parliament recommenced.

His early authorship added fluency and antithesis to his expression and a note of distinction to his name.

It developed his naturally historical point of view and prepared him for Reform, and for reforms. What is less obvious, but what I suspect is true, consists in that acquired susceptibility to the allurement of a phrase, an ailment to which Macaulay not seldom fell a victim. When Russell wrote of the voice of Wellington and Peel as the whisper of a faction, or of the religion of Roman Catholics as mummeries of superstition, he preferred the phrase to the fact. With an induced and disastrous clarity of thought he styled the war between North and South " a struggle on one side for empire and on the other for independence ".

VI

Latest but most protracted among the influences which helped to form him was the House itself, and that turbid sea of party which often wears away the finer surfaces of character.

Mill declared it to be the character of the British people, or at least of the enfranchised of Russell's day, " that to induce them to approve of any change, it is necessary that they should look upon it as a middle course." By birth and by conviction Russell was a Whig, holding a middle way between the Radicals, who, as he held, did not sufficiently esteem the Constitution, and the Tories, who did not sufficiently esteem liberty, civil and religious.

To the Whig party he was devoted all his life. Its aim, he declared in old age, " has always been my aim—the cause of civil and religious liberty all over the world. I have endeavoured, in the words of Lord Grey, to promote that cause without endangering the prerogatives of the Crown, the privileges of the two Houses of Parliament, or the rights and liberties of the people."

Historically he was conscious of his derivation from Fox, and from his ducal uncle and father, Fox's firm supporters. Had their principles, he contends, prevailed during the half-century preceding his own political career (c. 1770–1820) " the country would have avoided the American War and the first French Revolutionary War, the rebellion in Ireland in 1798, and the creation of three or four hundred millions of National Debt ".

Upon Pitt he was ready to lay every difficulty that England had or would have. " However, one has the satisfaction of thinking that a country which has survived being governed by Pitt must last for ever."

Yet he defended Pitt against the charge of being " an enemy to extended commerce and religious freedom ", and brought the charge of positive retrogression against his unworthy successors of 1816.

The principles of the " New Whigs " had pledged them, he maintained—(1) not to interfere in the

internal government of other countries ; (2) to
grant independence to America and political equality to Ireland ; (3) to promote religious liberty,
and to remove the political disabilities affecting
dissenters and Roman Catholics ; (4) to favour
parliamentary reform and liberty of the press.
During and after the war, the adherents of these
principles suffered an almost interminable exile
from influence and general approbation, a fact
which in part explains the amazing prominence of
Russell in his earlier parliamentary years. The
long delay in the adaptation of our forms and laws
to a largely transformed society, however, produced a condition of affairs which made the arguments of the reformers irresistible. And it may
well be that the chief historical importance of
Russell lies in his Whig, that is middle, position,
and that the aristocratic constitutionalist reformer,
with " somewhat of a superstitious reverence " for
the old system, was ideally fitted to be the lightning-
conductor of the gathered storm.

What his principles demanded when he entered
public life was nothing less than the reform of
" our foreign policy, our financial system, our
commercial exclusions, our intolerant laws, and
our parliamentary representation ". He was then
barely of age ; his health threatened to exclude
him from Parliament ; he was devoted to foreign
travel ; and he was soon to be writing a book a

year. Yet after some fifteen years Grey, his leader, considered that he had done more than any other living man.

VII

What he had done while still on the sunny side of forty was fourfold. (1) He had proved that with him principle came first, and that he would never surrender principle, whether to the tempting offer of Castlereagh, the menace of the King, the majestic appeal of Canning, or the politic advice of his party leaders. His principles were displayed whenever he spoke, whether against the compulsory transfer of the Norwegians to the Crown of Sweden, or of the French to the Bourbon line, or of Greek islanders to the Turks, or the suspension of the civil security of the English, or the danger to the Constitution that a vast standing army must involve, or the danger no less great if the new England of the factory and of the coalfield were denied a place within the Constitution. Inspired in part by his travels in the north of England as well as on the Continent, he was already realising that " it is from the great towns that light must proceed ". (2) By study, by diligent attendance, and by frequent and fearless intervention in debate, he had made himself a House of Commons man of the best type. (3) He had grasped the fact that the only safe road to reforms was by Reform, and that the representation of the people must not remain a mockery and a scandal. By frequent motions for the disfranchisement of rotten boroughs, for the enfranchisement of large towns, and for the suppression of electoral corruption, he had linked his name with the notion of Parliamentary Reform. And in his own mind he had determined that no mere palliatives would suffice, but that the change must conform to principles, however violent the breach with the past. (4) Curiously enough, if judged by the modern standard of party discipline, he and his principles gained several signal triumphs while the Tories ruled. Grampound was at least disfranchised, even if ministers took the road to their own destruction by refusing to assign its seats to Leeds. The Electors of Grampound, Russell learned, had been much improved by being driven to honest labour, and by 1822, " with the exception of one profligate alderman, became . . . scarcely to be recognised as the same persons ". In 1826, Russell's Anti-Bribery Bill was carried by the Speaker's casting vote.

Although against his will Jews remained under disabilities, the Test and Corporation Acts against Protestant Dissenters were repealed. The year 1829 witnessed the triumph of Catholic emancipation, Parliament and almost every office ceasing to be Protestant preserves.

Next year, as all the world knows, the Ministry

which was committed to oppose Reform foundered, and Russell's hour had come. He was one of four persons entrusted by Grey with the preparation of a Bill. Some 40 lbs. weight of calculations in his handwriting survive to attest his zeal. The draft was his, and, far more important, the determination to be logical rather than modest came from him. The Reform Bill of 1831, designed not to tinker with the question but to abolish it, achieved its immediate purpose by so capturing the imagination of the millions that the vested interests dared not inflexibly oppose.

Sixteen months of convulsion proved too much for Russell's physique; but they made his name. He emerged a Cabinet Minister and the hero of vast masses to whom he had previously been quite unknown. Three years later, early in 1835, his elder brother, no biased critic, could thus address him : " Your principles are clear as the sun at noonday. Of our leading statesmen you alone are intelligible. . . . Go on, my dear John, . . . and save your country ". The very clearness of Russell's principles reveals his limitations regarding Reform, of which he was the hero. It was much, it was indeed invaluable to his country, that he should have seen that Peel was wrong in holding that the voice of the people was already heard enough. He realised that, apart from precedent, property had its rights, and that, if votes were

given to half a million propertied Englishmen,
England might the better call on them to uphold
her. But he never took his stand " upon the broad
principle that the enfranchisement of capable
citizens, be they few or be they many—and if they
be many, so much the better—is an addition to
the strength of the State ". There is truth in the
nickname of " Finality Jack ". Russell never
wearied in bringing in new Reform Bills, but these
resembled the trifling additions to a great invention
advanced by an original and jealous patentee. He
remained a loyal Whig, when perhaps the Whig
mission was exhausted. " Universal suffrage ", he
early declared and always believed, " is the grave
of all temperate liberty, and the parent of tyranny
and licence."

VIII

The three years between the passing of the
Great Reform Bill and March 1835, when Russell's
brother urged him to save his country, had witnessed many startling changes. First the Whigs
gained in 1833 a vast though composite majority
in the Commons, and used it, among many lesser
reforms, to abolish slavery, to pass the first effective
Factory Act, and to amend the Poor Law. Irish
grievances, however, survived Emancipation, and
displayed Russell as a member of a Cabinet over
which another man presided. In October 1833,

finding that the majority did not propose to go as
far as he wished in reforming and reducing the
Irish Church, he wrote to Grey : " You have to
govern by military law in order . . . that the incomes
of the Church should be devoted exclusively to
the use of one-tenth of the population "—and
offered his resignation. This, it appeared, would
have threatened the downfall of the Ministry, and
by their downfall " probably war in Europe ".
Lord Holland, acting as a court of honour, defined
Russell's doubt in Russell's own manner as being
" whether, consistently with your principles and
honour, you can remain in a Ministry who propose
a measure short of that to which your opinions and
wishes would lead you, merely because it was
impracticable ". Russell remained, but in May
1834 " upset the coach " by publicly insisting that
justice to Ireland demanded that Parliament should
direct the appropriation of surplus Irish tithes to
public uses. The Irish question installed Melbourne
in place of Grey at the head of a weakened ministry
of Whigs, and Russell's inflexible demand for justice
to Ireland brought the King to dismiss a Premier
who wished to make him leader of the House of
Commons. Peel, hastening from Rome, held the
reins for a few months, but in April 1835 Russell
and Appropriation triumphed. A victory gained by
union between Whigs, Radicals, and Irish was
followed by the establishment of Melbourne as

Premier, with Russell as his Home Secretary and right-hand man. For seventeen years, divided almost equally between the ministries of Melbourne, of Peel, and of himself, Russell led his party in the Commons.

The first decade of these seventeen years, that is, from the reinstatement of Melbourne until Peel's declaration against the Corn Laws, is that of Russell's prime. In it he made his mark as the holder of two great offices of State. Year by year, as the strength of his Government declined, his own strength rose. Facing almost alone a formidable array of gladiators, Peel, Stanley, and Graham amongst them, he swiftly acquired and maintained the fame of a splendid parliamentary leader. He invariably raised the tone of a debate and diffused his rich stores of solid information and high principle within and without the Commons. He improved the laws of England both by positive enactments and by creating a moral atmosphere in which bad laws could not easily survive. And all this he did despite precarious health and a stunning domestic misfortune ; despite a lukewarm Premier, usually intractable followers, and an always hostile House of Lords.

" The succeeding generation, say from 1840 to 1870, practically lived upon the thought and sentiment of the seven or eight years immediately preceding the close of the Liberal reign in 1841."

And in generating such thought and sentiment during these years what parliamentary leader could compare with Russell ? Such generalisations as Cobden's in 1850, that Russell and the Whigs had been steadily losing ground since the Reform Bill, may be met by a simple statement of what, under none too favourable conditions, he accomplished. Justice to Ireland, it is true, was in part denied by the invincible resolution of the Lords. But Russell's boldness and firmness had exposed the anomaly of a State Church which in 150 parishes had not a single adherent. Although for the time being no more than a Poor Law Act and a Tithes Commutation Act could be passed, the exposure remained, and the Lords had carried through the dangerous achievement of defying not only the Commons but the report of a Royal Commission. In England Russell and his friends struck at a whole row of time-dishonoured abuses. The Municipal Reform Act of 1835 destroyed for ever the power of small bodies of freemen to sell to one another at dishonest prices the lands and other property of the corporations. If many church grievances remained, at least tithes were placed upon a rational footing, clerical absenteeism condemned, and Nonconformists allowed to marry outside buildings which they might quite sincerely regard as given over to idols. Legal punishments were made milder and more rational ; a great

University established on the basis of religious
freedom ; popular education championed ; public
health promoted ; cheap postage introduced. Becoming Colonial Secretary in 1839, Russell rendered
priceless services to the Empire. Between September 1841 and November 1845, as leader of a
disunited and impotent Opposition against Peel,
he advanced his reputation for dignity, capacity,
and Liberalism. On the burning question of
Ireland he declared for a complete equality
between Roman Catholics, Anglicans, and Pres-
byterians. He had the courage to support the
limitation of the hours of labour in factories.
Most important of all, his arguments aided the
growing Liberalism of Peel at the moment when
the Anti-Corn Law League had organised a great
and growing volume of popular opinion. The Tory
leader had already resolved in favour of repeal when
Russell, without consulting his followers, wrote
from Edinburgh to his constituents in the city of
London, " Observation and experience have convinced me that we ought to abstain from all
interference with the supply of food ". It is characteristic that in calling upon public opinion to
influence the Government he described " the struggle
to make bread scarce and dear " as " strong in
property, strong in the construction of our legislature, strong in opinion, strong in ancient associations, and the memory of immortal services ".

The result of this interference was that, after one of the most breathless chapters in our history, free trade in corn triumphed and Peel lay at Russell's mercy. The Whigs joined with the die-hard Protectionists to overthrow the Government, and at fifty-four Russell became Prime Minister.

IX

" Lord John's first premiership ", writes Dr. Gooch, " represents the culmination of his career ". The years 1846 to 1852 certainly appear as its watershed. They prove that when occupying the first place in the State Russell was as coolly courageous as in any other, and that to his principles he was, as ever, true. Few periods, moreover, have taxed courage and principle more severely. Famine in Ireland, financial panic in England, revolution abroad, threatened revolution at home, followed in swift succession. The Premier had no disciplined majority in the Commons ; to the Lords his principles were odious ; he was continually embarrassed by the attacks of the Court upon his conduct of foreign affairs. It was therefore no small achievement that Britain not only passed safely over the most treacherous of what Russell rightly called " these quicksand times ", but that she emerged with her Empire enlarged and strengthened and her laws in some respects improved. But it would

M

be difficult to meet the criticism that Russell's
too astute tactics in overthrowing Peel on Coercion
in 1846 were tacitly censured when he himself had
to coerce in 1847 ; that his talents were inadequate
to deal with the financial crisis ; that he showed
no mastery of the famine problem ; that a ten-
hours Bill and a Bill for improving the health of
towns were a miserable contribution to the con-
dition-of-the-people question ; that the dismissal
of Palmerston was a *coup d'état* ; and the Ecclesiastical Titles Act a crowning folly. At some
point between the Edinburgh Letter of 1845 and
the Durham Letter of 1850 the boundary is passed
which divides the Russell who was perhaps a great
statesman from the Russell who was certainly a
noble patriot and an eminent party-leader but
perhaps nothing more. The reason, who shall
confidently determine ? The greater strain of an
expanding and more complex world, the loss of
the steadying moral influence of Peel, the counsels
of his wife, the debasing influence of party struggles,
the increased arbitrariness often visible in ageing
men—any or all of these might account for the
restlessness and diminished power which mark
the succeeding stage of his career. By 1858 his
brother the Duke of Bedford was accustomed to
burn his letters immediately, so as to safeguard
his fame against the record of such foolishness
and injustice. "As to Lord John", wrote our

Ambassador from Paris in 1860, "one never knows where one is with him", and the disease poisoned the remainder of his political life. From his first premiership onwards, perhaps from his accession to the foremost place, he rendered, it is true, from time to time great services to his country, but at the price of blunders which may have overbalanced the account.

One such blunder was Russell's acceptance in 1852 of the post of Foreign Secretary for a few weeks. The "Who-Who?" Government under Derby had fallen by a majority of nineteen cast against Disraeli's budget at a moment when a general election had made the rule of any single party impossible. The outcome was a coalition of Whigs and Peelites under the aged Aberdeen, a coalition which could at least fill the great offices with very able men, while numbering a nominal majority of over fifty in the Commons. About eight-ninths of the combined forces, however, were in some sense followers of Russell, a fact which marked him out as Leader of the House and also as Premier expectant. To combine the leadership with a great office would overtax his strength; while to hold the leadership without having taken office of some kind was thought to be hardly in accordance with the constitution. Sinecure office he deemed unworthy. A solution was found in his appointment as Foreign Secretary, but only until Parliament should meet.

The post of Foreign Secretary had become one of intense and continuous labour on every day throughout the whole of the year. Palmerston assured the Prince Consort that the conferences alone occupied some four hours on every weekday. Red boxes containing the reports of our diplomatists abroad pursued the Secretary in an unbroken stream. In 1852, 32,043 despatches were received and sent out. An important ambassador, moreover, would think it suspicious if he did not hear privately from his chief at least once a week. Clarendon, emancipated from red boxes by a journey to Scotland on business, devoured the *Edinburgh Review* in the train, and said that during his four years in office he had not had such a lark. The post demanded robust health, business method, bonhomie and tact, besides ability and knowledge. In these last Russell was eminent, but his father had divined his want of judgment; his wife was compelled to confess that "he had no order or method in the arrangement of his papers"; and his staff found it difficult to secure his attention to minor duties. Above all, a country handicapped in its foreign relations by general elections unknown to the great autocracies of Europe needed the maximum of continuity that the parliamentary system would allow. England, thanks in no small degree to Russell, had had three Foreign Secretaries within a year. He now proceeded to raise the total to five in fourteen months, and this although in Clarendon the country possessed a diplomat and statesman who, by Bismarck's admission, might have prevented the Franco-Prussian War.

Russell took over the seals of office in December 1852, with the thousand difficulties of ministry-making and session-planning not yet fully overcome. At once the red boxes began to reveal a stormy and troubled Europe and a New World which threatened to disturb the balance of the Old. Had France guaranteed Cuba to Spain ? Could the United States be brought to renounce all designs upon it ? Was war avoidable between France and Russia ? How might the Latins and the Greeks be reconciled in Jerusalem ? What chastisement should be administered to the Reef pirates in Morocco ? people, as the Sultan said, " not under control . . . thus it has been from ancient times ". Could the Montenegrins be protected against the Turks and isolated from Austria, and were they rebels as well as marauders, or an independent race ? What could Britain do for the unruly subjects of Austria at Milan ? or for her persecuted neighbours in Switzerland ? or for the Protestant propagandists imprisoned in Tuscany ? and how could she at once protect Piedmont and restrain the violence of the Turin press ? British trade, as usual, needed

defence at this moment, notably in France and
Tunis. How further might Monaco be disposed
of ? and Chandernagore and Masulipatam ? and
the throne of Greece supported ? and that of
Denmark guarded against dispute ? On the
American mainland, was it the dishonesty of
Mexico or the stealthy aggression of the United
States that most demanded British vigilance or
action ? And how were the few remaining constitutional States in Europe to be protected against
the flowing tide of absolutism that had just
submerged the French ?

Amid this welter, two problems stood out with
especial boldness—the defence of the existing
territorial circumscription of Europe, and the
maintenance of peace. And the danger, as masses
of manuscript arriving every day attested, lay in
the hypothetical designs of two Emperors, Napoleon
and Nicholas of Russia. Napoleon, inscrutable by
reputation, as his sudden and amazing marriage
with the Spaniard Eugénie proved, we could in-
terrogate and generally spy upon day by day.
Twenty despatches came from our Paris Embassy
every week and supplementary letters doubtless
in proportion. Russell's principles at once found
application to the case of France. He risked
giving offence to Russia, Austria, and Prussia by
refraining from presenting to Napoleon the memorandum drawn up with them to warn him to be

quiet, and Britain declined to make any difficulty
about styling him Napoleon " the Third ". Russell
frankly admitted that he might naturally wish
to arm sufficiently to guard himself against the formidable power which Britain had displayed against
his uncle. But French preparations, he insisted,
formed a ground for similar action by Britain,
especially since steam had transformed the problem of defence. It was to the interest of France,
he sincerely and characteristically declared, that
Britain should be strong to maintain the peace of
Europe. He stood firm upon the boundary treaties
of the past, and warned France that any attempt
" to destroy the representative constitutions of
Spain or Portugal in form, substance or spirit "
would challenge war.

As a self-crowned adventurer and the lord of
an enormous army, Napoleon could not fail to
arouse the suspicions of a Power of which his subjects proclaimed their hate. And the Foreign
Secretary's difficulty in dealing with France was
increased by the fact that her policy might proceed
either from her Foreign Office or from Napoleon's
Cabinet, or from the department of the interior,
or from the department of police, two departments
eager for the overthrow of constitutional government wherever it might be found. The embarrassed
state of the French money-market favoured peace,
but many besides our diplomats at Paris held that

" the Emperor will sooner or later have to choose
between concession and war, between liberty and
glory ". It was the plain duty of a British Foreign
Secretary to preserve, if possible, the peace of
Europe unbroken ; to see to it that if Napoleon
were driven to war it should not be war with us ;
that if war came with us, we should be neither
unarmed nor lacking in allies.

X

At the moment, however, the danger of war
seemed to come from the other end of Europe. The
two crutches upon which Napoleon leaned were the
Army and the Church. To strengthen the latter,
and perhaps to gratify the thirst of the former for
prestige, he had made peremptory demands of the
Ottoman masters of Jerusalem. Latin aggression
had roused the Greeks, and the natural champion
of the Greek religion was the Tsar. Ominous signs
appeared that Nicholas thought that the time for
the dismemberment of the Turkish Empire had
come, and that Austria was his accomplice. From
the first days of Russell's tenure of the Foreign
Office, reports of military movements in the East
and French appeals to Britain poured in in a steady
stream. They were reinforced by the gloomy
language held to our ambassador by the Russian
Chancellor, Nesselrode, and by the suspicious

change of motive assigned by Russia in her instructions to her ambassador in London. If the movement of troops towards the Danube was justified first by the alleged misconduct of Turkey, and afterwards by the violence of France, the true cause was probably neither of the two. " My persuasion ", wrote Russell to Paris on January 5, however, " is that no project to dismember any part of the Turkish Empire will be entertained by Russia without a previous communication to England and France ". On the 25th, addressing Petersburg, he expressed his " well-founded " hope that the Tsar would stay his hand, pointing out at the same time the danger of provoking the hot spirits among the French army.

On January 28 he sent to Paris a solemn warning against the violence at Jerusalem which he regarded as the origin of the strife. It was " melancholy indeed ", he declared, " to see rival Churches contending for mastery in the very place where Christ died for mankind ", and foolish for France and Russia to show up the weakness of the Sultan. This despatch is an excellent example of Russell's noble confidence in the power of truth to prevail, and of his naïve confidence in himself as its exponent. Napoleon perhaps might be susceptible to such an appeal and capable of recognising an honest statesman. For several years to come his English contemporaries found the Emperor eminently

straightforward. But in Russian eyes Russell was
" not bad but . . . sly ", delighting to see Aberdeen struggling with Austria in Italy and with
Russia in Turkey, and to the Tsar our honesty
was unintelligible. While he exhorted France
and Russia, Russell was warning the Sultan
to act promptly in self-defence by accepting
for Jerusalem whatever arrangements these two
Powers might agree on, by adopting a merely
defensive attitude with regard to Montenegro, and
in general by improving the government of those
dominions in which his power was unquestioned.
On January 29 he replied immediately to a despatch
received from Paris " containing matter of very
serious import ". This transmitted an appeal
from the French Foreign Minister, Drouyn de
L'huys, that England would consider the question
of the preservation of the Turkish Empire in all its
bearings, and would collaborate with France. It
was the weakness of Turkey, Russell declared, that
made France and Russia suspect each other, but
" Her Majesty's Government are persuaded that
the Emperor of Russia will not enter willingly, and
certainly not without the consent of England, into
any schemes for the subversion of the Ottoman
Power. Her Majesty's Government have reasons
quite satisfactory to them for this persuasion."
And having already prescribed to Russia, France
and Turkey, Russell next prescribed to Austria

with regard to Montenegro. The turn of the United States came, as we have seen, a little later. Thus in eight weeks of office Russell taught nearly as many Powers their duty.

Ten days after Russell had written with serene confidence that the Tsar would not assail Turkey without the consent of England, the precise instructions by which Menshikov was to summon the Sultan to surrender were formally written down. The warnings of the French were thus proved true ; Britain had been palpably and painfully befooled ; in little more than a year the Crimean struggle was to begin. The fault in so far as it was Russell's lay rather in his acceptance of a post for which he was unfit than in failure to do his best. The least diplomatic of men, he was doubtless proofed against mere hints of the Tsar's purpose by his reliance on the agreement drawn up by Nesselrode in 1844, and known also to Palmerston and Aberdeen. This pledged the parties to maintain Turkey as long as possible, but, in words dictated by the Tsar, " if we foresee that it must crumble to pieces, to consult together as to everything relating to the establishment of a new order of things ". The Tsar and Nesselrode now repeatedly indicated that the crumbling was imminent, but Russell and Aberdeen thought that they had disposed of the matter by replying that Turkey might last a great while longer and that interference might hasten the crumbling

which it was intended to prevent. The despatch
proving how England misjudged the situation was
read to the Tsar on February 21, the day on which
Russell transferred to Clarendon the seals of office.
It evoked merely an offer of partition, for the
Russian plan of campaign was already far advanced.
Russell had at least secured for his country a
demonstrable absence of guilt, and in prevailing
with Lord Stratford de Redcliffe to return to
Constantinople he had secured the treatment of the
question by the one Englishman who understood it.
During his short term of office, moreover, he had
strenuously upheld the rights of England as against
the United States, and of British subjects as against
the Austrian police. Civil and religious liberty all
over the world had indeed been his conspicuous
care, and his methods had been those with which
the world was to become familiar between 1859
and 1865.

XI

The thirteen remaining years of his political
prominence and remaining quarter of a century of
his life add in my opinion more to his notoriety
than to his fame. Had his career ended with the
repeal of the Corn Laws we should have lamented
the loss of a statesman whose long and brilliant
public service promised unbounded benefit to his
country if only he had become Prime Minister.

Had he retired in 1852 after his first premiership he would at least have enjoyed the added distinction of having seen England through some of the most difficult years in history, and of having sacrificed his political position to his love of her Protestant freedom. But those chapters in his life which record his connection with the Crimean War, his four years' wanderings in the wilderness, his appropriation and exercise of the Foreign Secretaryship, and his inglorious second premiership, reveal no new virtues and emphasise the old defects. His sole resplendent triumph, his contribution to united Italy, has been brilliantly displayed by Mr. Trevelyan. A student who yields to the charm of a character of rare and noble beauty and to the fascinating record of an aged statesman's domestic life will pass as lightly as may be over the years of political decline. Of the Roebuck motion, and Poland, and Slesvig-Holstein, and the *Alabama*, we will say here and now what some kindly cynics bid us say of all ancient history—let bygones be bygones.

But it remains for me, not forgetting that these events happened, to attempt some estimate of Russell's place in history. He was, I believe, not merely or chiefly a " notable Prime Minister " but a really eminent man. It was not for nothing that so judicious a historian as Mr. Lecky wrote of his later years, "Beyond all men I have ever known, he had the gift of seizing rapidly in every question—the essential fact or distinction. . . . I have never met with any one with whom it was so possible to discuss with profit many great questions in a short time." The total impression left upon my mind by a mass of contemporary evidence is that while many men might grumble at the vagaries and failings of " Johnny ", his intellect and principles alike commanded a rare respect. Therefore his lapses never ruined him for long, and this least meretricious and demagogic of party leaders became Premier a second time a quarter of a century after he had first supplanted Peel. But granted that Russell was eminent, may we go further and pronounce him great ? Before answering, if it is not cowardly, I would plead for further time. It would be rash to assign a place in history when barely sixty years have passed since the hero's abdication. Russell, as his intimates declared, was unlike any one else—a strange compound of a giant and a child ; and his career is likewise full of contradictions. He was the only man who could lead his party in the Commons, yet he brought the Whigs to extinction. His principles were redolent of internationalism, yet he habitually sought peace in the shadow of the sword. He served his country in many capacities for many years, but it may be true that he sometimes deprived her of the services of better men. The supreme difficulty seems to lie in his peculiai relation to democracy, itself perhaps an ambiguous institution. In 1831 he undoubtedly advanced it, arousing in part the appetite which his Bill appeased. Thereafter he regarded himself as the patentee of Reform, in his hands an attenuated medicine. Instead of the sound adult population voting in secret, Russell set as his ideal males of at least moderate property and education voting in public. He thus—at least until the national education which he championed should bear fruit— founded the franchise on material possessions and repudiated to the end of his life the principle that since we are men, not snails, it is manhood, not ratepaying, that should qualify for the vote. Whether in this he was merely limited or supremely wise the future must determine.

No less difficult is a final decision on the charge that he failed to grasp the importance of a still more vital question—that of the condition of the people. No one can deny that his principles favoured social improvement and that he effected or attempted not a few reforms. The history in our own day of such simple and obvious benefits as summer time and a fixed Easter may well remind us that custom is still a mighty force. His power, moreover, was never to be measured by the numbers of his nominal supporters. Legislation affecting property tended to resolve the Liberal party into its constituent Radicals and Whigs and to expose change to the veto of the yet unchallenged Lords. Nowhere could Russell's trenchant tongue and pen have been more victoriously employed than in exposing social abuses. From the point of view of parliamentary tactics, however, this would have been the wrong course and he did not take it. In thus abstaining from a crusade because he lacked conviction he was no more and no less than representative of his age and of his class. Had he been in advance of them his attitude towards democracy must have altered, for only the representatives of the masses would modify property to their advantage.

Russell's title to greatness, then, must rest upon the unique services that he rendered to his own country in 1831 and to Italy in 1860, together with a possible future verdict of history to the effect that the progressive party from 1832 to 1866 needed a rein and not a spur. To deny him greatness is not to deny him eminence in the proud position of a public man. It was given to him upon his deathbed to write his own epitaph with his accustomed clarity and truth—" I have made mistakes, but in all I did my object was the public good ".

BENJAMIN DISRAELI, EARL OF BEACONSFIELD

By F. J. C. HEARNSHAW

I

SOME months ago, when I was first contemplating the preparation of this lecture, I picked up in a second-hand book-store a curious and interesting volume entitled *The Right Honourable Benjamin Disraeli, M.P. : A Literary and Political Biography.* It is an anonymous production, dated 1854, and published by the eminently respectable Richard Bentley, publisher in ordinary to Her Majesty. The work claims to be the first attempt to write the life of Disraeli, and the claim is probably valid. For Disraeli was at that date but fifty years old ; he had never climbed up the greasy pole to a point higher than the office of Chancellor of the Exchequer, and he was at the moment merely the leader of a hopeless and disgruntled Opposition. He had still twenty-seven years of strenuous toil and varied achievement before him, of which the writer of this peculiar volume had not the remotest inkling. It was probably of this very monument of premature anticipation of the day of judgment that Disraeli was thinking when he said to Mr. T. E. Kebbel in 1860, " I disapprove of contemporary biography, and I dislike being the subject of it ". For this anonymous study, though well written and excellently produced, is an unmeasured and unmitigated attack on Disraeli from the Peelite point of view. It accuses him, throughout its six hundred pages, of having no principles, no intelligence, and no virtue. The book made some sensation at the time of its appearance, and its authorship was much canvassed. Lord Lyndhurst called it " a very blackguard publication " and suspected the youthful Sir William Harcourt of having written it. Ultimately, however, it was traced to a certain Thomas MacKnight, a budding journalist of twenty-five years of age, who for two sessions (1849-51) had been a student of King's College, and, during the latter portion of his time, president of the Literary and Scientific Union of the College. I mention this fact because it seems appropriate that, after seventy-two years, King's College should revise its estimate of Disraeli. This lecture, of course, can make no pretence to furnish any material contribution to such a revision. The task lies in the capable hands of the venerable Sir Edward Clark, a student of King's College only ten years after Thomas MacKnight himself, and later a Member of Parliament while still Disraeli was Prime Minister. His forthcoming *Life of Lord Beaconsfield* is eagerly awaited.[1]

The second chapter of Mr. MacKnight's philippic begins with the words : " The year 1826 must be a remarkable one in English annals " ; and the reason that Mr. MacKnight gives for this opinion shows that, however much he may disapprove of Disraeli, he clearly recognises his greatness. For the reason why the year 1826 will be remarkable in English annals is simply and solely that Disraeli then began his public career. It was the year—of which the present year is the centenary—that saw the appearance (January 25) and the disappearance (July 29) of the independent Tory newspaper, *The Representative*, which Disraeli projected and persuaded John Murray to take up. It was the year which witnessed (April 18) the publication of Disraeli's first and most sensational novel, *Vivian Grey* (Part I.)—a novel of a new type which at once succeeded in its main purpose, viz. that of making its author notorious. It was the year which (in the autumn) for the first time took him abroad, and, in a three months' tour, revealed to him a new world of cities and men—a world whose fascinating affairs called him irresistibly away from the life of literature to the life of action.

---

[1] This volume has been published by Mr. John Murray during the passage of these sheets through the press.

II

At the opening of this cardinal year, 1826,
Benjamin Disraeli had just come of age. He was
living with his father, Isaac, the well-known man
of letters, in a house full of books, at the corner
of Bloomsbury Square and Hart Street, in the
vicinity of the British Museum—a house still ex-
tant and in externals little changed, although in-
ternally no longer a library but a nest of offices.
Born of Jewish parents (December 21, 1804), he
had been duly circumcised into the synagogue.
But Isaac, who had early been fascinated by
Voltaire, had ceased to be a Jew in religion, and in
1817 he withdrew himself and his family from the
communion of his people. Thus the way was
opened for Benjamin's baptism into the Christian
Church (July 31, 1817), a prudential move recommended by the profligate Samuel Rogers, and ac-
quiesced in by the indifferent Isaac as one without
which the path to public life would be barred to
the boy. Up to that date Benjamin's education
had been second-rate and unsystematic, and although after his conversion into a Christian he was
able to go to a better school (Rev. Eli Cogan's in
Epping Forest) he never made up for lost oppor-
tunities, and he remained deficient both in exact
scholarship and in the scientific attitude of mind.
This was not wholly a disadvantage. What he lost

in erudition he gained in individuality. It suited his powerful and original genius to browse in his father's immense book-store, to let his imagination work at leisure, to follow his own adventurous lines of thought. He escaped the permanent infantile paralysis which is often the consequence of a public school curriculum; he evaded the premature senile decay that is sometimes the painful sequel to a university career. So remarkable, indeed, were the native powers which he developed that in 1825 Murray wrote to Lockhart, the son-in-law and biographer of Sir Walter Scott, " I may frankly say that I never met with a young man of greater promise . . . he is worthy of any degree of confidence that you may be induced to repose in him ".

He was fully conscious of his abilities, and he was consumed with a passion to make a name, win renown, govern men, and stamp an impress on his age. On his leaving school (1821), his father had apprenticed him to the law, but he had broken away from the legal career as one that allowed no scope for his peculiar gifts. He felt that he was born to rule ; to mould the ideas of his generation ; to dominate the wills of his contemporaries ; to influence the course of the world's concerns. Only two careers offered the necessary scope—literature and politics. Of these two, without question, politics from the very first displayed superior attractions. *Vivian Grey*—an intimately autobiographic study—reveals a youth to whom parliament, leadership, office, and ultimate prime ministry present the only path of life worth pursuing. But, unfortunately, while literature may be a mode of earning money, politics is (for a beginner) merely a mode of spending it. And Disraeli was impecunious. No doubt, if he had been a young man of Scottish parentage, content to plod on porridge, the allowance made him by his father would have been adequate. Long years of diligent obscurity would have been rewarded by a respectable competence in some out-of-the-way corner of the great world. But Disraeli's overmastering ambition, his sense of sovereign power, his conviction of high destiny dependent only on his courage and his will, demanded an immediate freedom of a kind entirely incompatible with straitened means. He needed a lot of money and he needed it at once. For about a dozen years (1826–37) he depended primarily on the produce of his pen. He wrote books and articles which on the one hand were likely to pay, and on the other hand to make his name notorious. He became widely known in the literary world as " Disraeli the younger ", and he earned considerable sums, but not nearly enough. Hence he, further, speculated on the Stock Exchange ; but, as he did so with imperfect knowledge and insufficient caution, the results were so disastrous that he was speedily compelled to refrain. He then ran deeply into debt, and got painfully involved in the meshes of the money-lenders and the complexities of the bankruptcy courts. Finally, he found escape into the clear air by means of marriage with a wealthy widow (1839), with whom he subsequently fell in love, and in whose company he spent thirty-three years of a singularly happy wedded life.

III

The years 1826–37, which saw Disraeli's emergence into literary fame and his protracted struggle with financial embarrassment, witnessed also his early and unsuccessful attempts to enter parliament. Three times he stood as an Independent for High Wycombe (1832–34) and once as a Tory for Taunton (1835). As a candidate for parliament he was hampered not only by his poverty, but also by his name and race, and by the extreme uncertainty of his political position. Of his name and race he was so immensely proud that he could do no more and no less than defy prejudice, denounce persecution, and defend the reputation of his people. As to his political position, the case was not so simple. He found himself out of sympathy with both the great parties of the period. With the Whigs he could have absolutely nothing to do. He detested them as the enemies of the

Crown, the subverters of the Church, the exploiters of the people. He regarded them as a selfish and anti-national oligarchy engaged at the moment in trying to establish for themselves a permanent ascendancy in the country, based on the dominantly middle-class franchise of the Reform Bills of 1830–1832. On the other hand, the Tories, with whom were his natural affinities, were in a condition of disintegration and despair. Their unity had been shattered by the Catholic Emancipation question in 1829 ; they had been annihilated in the struggle over the Reform Bills of 1830–32. They had no policy, no outlook, no future. Under Wellington their sole idea was to oppose all change, whether bad or good, as long as possible, and, when resistance was no longer feasible, to retreat to the next obstructive position. They were a party of elderly obscurantists devoid alike of energy and hope. Disraeli could not doom himself to despondency and death by joining them in 1832—the date of their deepest depression.

From the moment of his entry into politics his individuality and originality were marked. Even as a youth it was for him to formulate policies, not to accept them ; to construct parties, not to join them. He presented himself to the electors of High Wycombe as an Independent opponent of the Whigs, and he called upon all opponents of the Whigs—whether Tory, or Radical, or Nationalist—

to rally to his aid. His nomination was proposed
by a Tory, seconded by a Radical, and supported
by letters from the Reformer Joseph Hume and
the Irish Nationalist Daniel O'Connell. His programme, replete with measures intended to break
the power of the Whig oligarchy and bring to an
end the ascendancy of the middle classes, was
composed of items drawn from multifarious sources,
including his own vivid imagination. No wonder
the bewildered electors asked "What is he?"
And no wonder that, failing to receive an answer
which they could understand, they rejected him.

In 1834 he made the fateful acquaintance of
Lord Lyndhurst—Lord Chancellor under Canning,
Goderich, and Wellington, and soon to become
Lord Chancellor again under Sir Robert Peel.
Lyndhurst—who was much attracted by him and
profoundly impressed by his fascinating and powerful personality—succeeded in convincing him, first,
that it was useless to attempt anything in parliamentary politics except as a member of an
organised party ; and, secondly, that the Toryism
of Peel, as distinct from that of Wellington, held
the promise of the future. Disraeli, therefore, in
1835 gave his adhesion to Peel, accepted the Tamworth Manifesto, and stood as an avowed Tory for
Taunton. The contest, which was against a popular
minister seeking re-election on appointment to
office, was a hopeless one from the first ; but

Disraeli fought it with inimitable gusto and brilliance. Though beaten at the poll, he drew upon himself the attention of the whole country, partly by the novelty of his exposition of Tory principles, partly by the fury of an attack which he brought upon himself from his former Nationalist ally, O'Connell, who had now transferred his alliance to the hated Whigs. Disraeli's apparent inconsistency in seeking O'Connell's support in 1832 and describing him as a sanguinary traitor in 1835 called, indeed, urgently for explanation. Disraeli hastened to give it ; all the more rapidly because there was nothing upon which he prided himself more than upon his consistency, nothing about which he was more sensitive than any suggestion of laxity of principle. First, he defended himself in a series of terrific letters to the *Times*. Secondly, he expounded his fundamental political tenets, in the form of a long and elaborate epistle addressed to Lord Lyndhurst, under the title " A Vindication of the English Constitution " (1835). It is one of the most serious, thoughtful, and illuminating of all his political writings. Even now it is well worthy of careful study as a highly penetrating and original analysis of British institutions and ideas. It is redolent of the spirit of Bolingbroke and the principles of Burke. It condemns utilitarianism, philosophical radicalism, and all similar applications of abstract theory to practical politics.

It insists on the fundamental importance of tradition, custom, inheritance, national character, as a basis for constitutional progress. It commends the " wisdom of our ancestors ", who in all their conflicts, whether with tyrants or with anarchists, appealed rather to precedent than to dogma, and maintained the immemorial " Rights of Englishmen " rather than the imaginary " Rights of Man ". It defends the ancient prerogatives of the Crown ; the long-established powers of the House of Lords —an assembly as truly representative as the House of Commons itself ; the authority of the National Church ; the preponderance of the landed interest against the new commercialism ; the virtues and delights of the old tranquil England of gentry and peasantry as contrasted with the feverish agitations of the transmuted England of the merchants, manufacturers, mill - owners, mine - sinkers, and would-be millionaires of the money-grubbing middle-class.

IV

The death of William IV. and the consequent accession of Victoria in 1837 necessitated a general election, and at that election Disraeli at last found a seat as one of the two Tory members for Maidstone. It is an interesting coincidence that Disraeli's entry into Parliament should have exactly coincided with the beginning of the reign of the

Great Queen with whom his association was later to be so close. It is noteworthy also that both the character and ability of the new monarch made it much more easy for Disraeli to gain acceptance for his exalted conception of the royal prerogative than would have been the case if monarchy had continued to be represented either by the obscurantist and incapable William IV., or by any other of the " nasty old men " who claimed George III. as their progenitor.

From 1837 to the day of his death, forty-four years later, Disraeli was never out of Parliament : he represented Maidstone 1837–41, Shrewsbury 1841–47, Buckinghamshire 1847–76 ; in 1876 he went, as Earl of Beaconsfield, to the House of Lords. The first twelve years of this period (1837–49), during which his powers both as writer and debater reached their magnificent meridian, sufficed to establish him as leader of the Tory party. The story of this rapid rise to dominance is one of the most dramatic in our parliamentary history. For Disraeli did not, like Gladstone, rise by a smooth and gradual ascent, with the lavish assistance of kind patrons and wealthy borough-mongers, through minor offices and junior lordships, to eminence and power. He owed his advance to his own ability and character alone ; he had to fight for every step ; he had to overcome almost invincible prejudice, and to surmount a stubborn distrust which had

not unnaturally been generated both by the morals
of *Vivian Grey* and by the manifestos of his own
" independence " days. He had to storm the
citadel of sovereignty. The only office he ever
held before he became Prime Minister was that of
Chancellor of the Exchequer, with the leadership
of the House of Commons attached to it. To
attain this exalted place he had to overthrow Sir
Robert Peel, one of the most powerful ministers of
modern times ; to convert the Earl of Derby, who
began by regarding him as an unprincipled adventurer ; to supersede the Marquis of Granby,
whom rank and influence indicated as Peel's suc-
cessor ; to conciliate the Prince Consort, who disapproved of his behaviour in Parliament ; to
capture the Queen, who agreed with the Prince
Consort. His accomplishment of this complicated
operation was a triumph of skill, patience, courage,
and indomitable determination.

We can distinguish four stages in his ascent
from insignificance to supremacy during the twelve
years under review. For exactly one half of the
time (1837–43) he was the faithful and loyal
follower of Sir Robert Peel. He spoke and wrote
of him with enthusiasm as " the only hope of
England " ; upheld his cause in Parliament and
country ; voted for his measures, and defended
his policy with masterly dialectic. Yet even in this
period of party fidelity he showed traces of his old

Radical independence by pleading, against the
majority of his party, for more consideration for
the petitions of the Chartists, more mercy for their
misguided leaders, and less reliance on mere
repression. When Peel became Prime Minister in
1841 he would probably have rewarded Disraeli's
conspicuous services with some office or other, but
for the invincible resistance of the still unconverted
Derby (then Lord Stanley).

The year 1843 saw a change in Disraeli's attitude
towards his chief. He became critical ; he showed
dissatisfaction with Peel's policy ; he began to
suspect that the great administrator lacked
principles and ideas ; he allied himself with the
" Young England " party of George Smythe and
Lord John Manners, who wished to organise a great
crusade against the industrial revolution, and on
behalf of the " Old England " of active monarchy,
beneficent nobility, paternal clergy, and contented
peasantry. Thus he reverted to independence, and
to what he claimed to be the only genuine Toryism
—the Toryism of Wyndham and Bolingbroke, of
Chatham and Pitt—a Toryism which he had always
maintained and from which he would never swerve.
In his great novel *Coningsby* (1844) he set forth the
ideals of the " Young England " group, and
deplored the unprincipled opportunism of the new
Conservatism which consisted merely of " Tory
men and Whig measures ". In parliament, too,

he became formidable in his criticisms. Peel
found him hostile, though respectful, in such matters
as the administration of the new Poor Law, the
coercion of Ireland, and the conduct of policy
respecting the Near East.

In 1844 Peel, intensely irritated by Disraeli's
damaging dissent, and stirred to action by Sir
James Graham and other still more angry medio-
crities, threw down the gauntlet by withdrawing
the party whips and attempting to ostracise and
destroy the inconvenient critic. Never did misguided minister take a more fatal step. Disraeli,
now freed by his chief's own act from the ties of
allegiance, gave full vent to his profound dissatisfaction with the unprincipled and unimaginative Conservatism of the Cabinet, which he
ultimately roundly denounced as an " organised
hypocrisy ". Never since the remote days when
the elder Pitt had poured forth the vials of his
scorn upon the time-serving Walpole had the walls
of parliament echoed to such destructive sarcasm
or withering irony. The opening of Mazzini's
correspondence by the officials of the Post Office ;
the refusal of the Government to protect the
West-Indian sugar planters against the competition
of slave-owning rivals ; the grant to the Catholic
College of Maynooth—these, and many other
matters that raised fundamental questions of
principle, gave occasion for attacks made with

consummate skill and pressed home with inimitable vigour and resource. The climax, however, was not reached until, in January 1846, Peel
seemed to justify all Disraeli's taunts and accusations by abandoning the cause of the Corn Laws
which he had been specially placed in power to
defend, and by proclaiming himself a convert of
Cobden. Disraeli, in denouncing Peel's treachery,
found himself at last giving voice not merely to
his own sentiments, or to the opinions of a small
" Young England " group, but to the inarticulate
emotions of the immense majority of the outraged
"gentlemen of England " whom Peel had cajoled
and betrayed. Disraeli attempted no economic
defence of the Corn Laws. In so far as he defended
them at all, he did so on social and political grounds.
But he directed his energies and abilities primarily
to a deadly attack on Peel for violating his mandate,
for breaking his pledges, for deserting his followers,
for destroying confidence in the good faith of public
men, for shattering his party, for rendering parliamentary government impossible. He contended
with unanswerable logic that if the repeal of the
Corn Laws was indeed right and necessary, Cobden
and not Sir Robert was the person to effect the
change. He denied, however, both the right and
the necessity. Even though the Corn Laws were
but a means and not an end—a matter of expediency and not of principle—yet they were a

means to one of the most important of all ends,
viz. the maintenance of the landed interest in
England ; and they should not be revoked until
some other means had been found to ensure the
food supply of the nation in time of war, and the
continuance of that splendid race of English
country-folk by whom the greatness of England
had been achieved. He fought for the menaced
farm against the encroaching factory ; for the
vanishing village against the spreading slum ; for
the cause of agriculture against the industrial
revolution. On the specific issue, of course, he
was beaten. The coalition of Peelites, Whigs, and
Cobdenites carried the repeal of the Corn Laws.
But the victory of Peel was a Pyrrhic one. On the
very day (May 15, 1846) when the Corn Laws were
swept away, the Country Party had its revenge
on its renegade leader by combining with his
other enemies to defeat him on an Irish Coercion
Bill.

The fourth and last stage of this cardinal period
(1846–49) saw Disraeli gradually established in
undisputed leadership of the Country Party in
the House of Commons—the Earl of Derby being
its leader in the House of Lords. It was a slow and
laborious process. In spite of his brilliant services,
he had to overcome deep-seated prejudices against
his alien race, his lack of rank, his ambiguous
religion, his doubtful reputation. He was content

o

to work and wait, confident that in the end he
would command recognition. At first he loyally
served under the nominal leadership of Lord George
Bentinck. After Bentinck's sudden death in
September 1848, he was content to be one of a
nominal triumvirate, of which Granby and Herries
were the other members. But in 1849 pretences
were abandoned, and he was allowed to stand alone
as leader of the Opposition to Lord John Russell's
Whig government. Said the exiled French minister
Guizot to him at this date : " I think your being
leader of the Tory party is the greatest triumph
that Liberalism has ever achieved ". What Peel
thought of this triumph of Liberalism can be
better imagined than described.

V

The leadership of the shattered remnants of the
Tory party in the House of Commons in 1849 and
the following years was a by no means enviable
position. For exactly a quarter of a century, that
is until 1874, the party that Disraeli led was in a
permanent minority in parliament. Its attenuated
ranks were torn by dissensions, jealousies, and
intrigues, while ever and anon open rebellion
challenged its leader's authority. It was faced by
a powerful and malignant, if composite, majority—
by Whigs led by the capable Russell and the

popular Palmerston; by Radicals strong in the
victorious common-sense of Cobden and the terrific oratory of Bright; above all, by Peelites
held together, after Sir Robert's death in 1850,
by Graham and Gladstone, and burning with
inextinguishable fury against the man who had
hounded their great chief from public life. Three
times only in that long period was chronic opposition relieved by a brief tenure of office without
power, viz. 1852, 1858–59, 1867–68. In 1855, it is
true, at the crisis of the Crimean War, Derby had
the opportunity of taking office with an excellent
prospect of establishing his party in authority for
a prolonged period; but, with a levity and a
timidity which drove Disraeli almost to despair, he
made the great refusal, and condemned himself
and his disgusted followers to another long spell
of impotence. There is no doubt, in fact, that
Derby, the nominal head of his party, was the most
formidable obstacle that Disraeli ever had to surmount in the whole course of his upward career.
It was Derby who had prevented his entry into
office in 1841; it was Derby who delayed his
recognition as leader of the Country Party till
1849; it was Derby who criticised and obstructed
his budgets in 1852; it was Derby who for years
prevented him from educating the Tories away
from the hopeless cause of protection; finally,
it was Derby—a clever but frivolous amateur in

politics—who threw away all the results of six
years of Disraeli's magnificent work in the reconstruction of Toryism in the House of Commons,
by declining to form a ministry in 1855. It is
lamentable to think that Disraeli, as yet only
fifty-one years old, and still hardly past the summit
of his power, should by his leader's incredible
feebleness and folly have been doomed to nineteen
more years of exile, and have been denied office
with the power of a majority behind it until
(1874) he was old, broken in health, widowed, and
forlorn.

For twenty - five years, then, Disraeli led a
minority in the House of Commons. Within the
walls of parliament his great task—a slow and
toilsome one—was the education of his party : he
had to wean it from protection and to win it for
reform ; he had to elevate it from an exclusive
class - consciousness into a patriotic enthusiasm
for the people as a whole ; he had to inspire it
with zeal for social wellbeing, for national prestige,
and for imperial greatness. Outside the walls of
parliament, he had to persuade a majority of the
electorate that the only secure bases of prosperity
and progress are the venerable constitution gradually built up by the wisdom of our ancestors ; the
national Church with its official recognition of the
spiritual foundations of society, its wide inclusive-
ness, its large tolerance, its high scholarship ; the

traditions, customs, habits, and beliefs handed down to us from an immemorial antiquity.

There is, of course, in an essay like this no room to trace in detail the process by which he achieved his purposes and attained to the triumph of 1874. So early as 1852, when he became Chancellor of the Exchequer for ten months, he may be said to have weaned his party from protection. He got them to realise that when certain things, such as the repeal of the Corn Laws, have been done— whether for good or for ill—they cannot be undone. He taught them to seek the maintenance of the landed interest by other means than the impossible reimposition of the Corn Laws—by remission of taxation, by adjustments of poor rates, by repeal of malt duties, and so on. By 1867 he may be considered to have won his party for reform. The great Act of that year—which established household suffrage in towns, introduced the lodger franchise, and widely distributed seats—was a personal triumph of a unique kind. Agreeing with the Queen and with Lord Derby that a question that had agitated the country for fifteen years—a question that had defied half - a - dozen serious attempts at settlement—should at all costs be disposed of, he bent the whole powers of his mind and will to the colossal task of carrying his Bill. His party was, as ever since 1846, a minority of the House and many of its members were hostile

to any extension of the franchise. He was faced
by an envenomed majority, headed by Gladstone,
who were resolved by all conceivable means to
wreck the Bill and prevent the Tories from winning
the credit for solving the popular problem. The
way in which he kept together his friends and
baffled his foes is a miracle of parliamentary skill.
His success, in spite of defection and opposition,
filled Gladstone with a fury so intense that he
was stimulated to bring the disestablishment of
the Irish Church into the political arena, in order
that Disraeli might not reap at the polls the fruit
of his parliamentary triumph. Gladstone's clever
move—the most brilliant piece of strategy he ever
displayed in party warfare—undoubtedly delayed
Disraeli's capture of the country for six years.
He was beaten on the Irish Church question in the
General Election of 1868, and his great rival was
established in office with a large majority behind
him. The six years, however, of Gladstone's first
ministry were troubled and unprosperous. At
home they were marked by a perpetual agitation
that seemed to threaten every old-established institution of the country and many a venerable
interest. Abroad they were characterised by impotence and humiliation; the power of Britain
seemed to have vanished and to be negligible as
the Franco-Prussian war ran its course; the prestige of Britain appeared to be a thing of the past

when Russia, without consulting the signatories of the Peace of Paris, repudiated the Black Sea clauses of that settlement of 1856.

As Gladstone sank in popular esteem, Disraeli rose. In February 1872, when he rode through the streets of London on his return from the thanksgiving service held in St. Paul's to celebrate the recovery of the Prince of Wales from his serious illness, he was greeted by an ovation which showed him that he was on the eve of the great attainment. A visit which he paid to Manchester in April 1872 was an occasion of unprecedented enthusiasm, and the four hours' speech which he delivered in the Free Trade Hall proved to be an unequalled presentation of the Conservative creed as it had been formulated by his genius and instilled into his party during the long years of adversity. Still more spectacular was his triumph at the Crystal Palace in June of the same year. There again he made a speech which proclaimed far and wide the evangel of the Tory Democracy of which he was the genius and the pioneer—the maintenance of British institutions, the development and consolidation of the Empire, the elevation of the condition of the people. Disraeli's devoted and faithful wife (since 1868 Viscountess Beaconsfield) lived long enough to witness and to rejoice in these presages of impending victory. But, alas, before the consummation came—to his enduring grief—she was taken from his side. She died on December 15, 1872.

Next year Gladstone resigned ; but Disraeli refused to accept office in a Parliament in which he had no majority. Hence Gladstone had to carry on, amid growing dissatisfaction, until February 1874. Then the inevitable end came, and a general election gave Disraeli a majority of fifty over all other parties combined. At last his opportunity had come.

VI

His opportunity had come ! But, sad to say, he was too old, too weary, too much disillusioned, too seriously broken both in health and in spirits, to avail himself of it. Even in 1868, when on Derby's retirement he had been for a few months Prime Minister, he had remarked, " It is twenty years too late ! " and now another lustrum had elapsed, full of exhausting toils, overwhelming sorrows, and debilitating illnesses. He had become a victim to chronic asthma, bronchitis, and gout, and only with difficulty could he summon energy to toil through the necessary routine labours of the day. In the circumstances it is wonderful that he succeeded in achieving so much as he actually did during the six years of his Prime Ministry (1874–80).

He began unluckily by lending his support to

a Public Worship Regulation Act intended to keep
Ritualists obedient to their vows and to the law.
It was not his own measure, but one introduced
by the two Archbishops, supported by the majority
of the episcopal bench, and enthusiastically favoured
by the Queen. After much deliberation he decided
to give the measure that official furtherance without
which it could not have passed the two Houses.
He was thus regarded by the Ritualists as responsible for it ; and they, while repudiating its
authority, and defying its penalties, turned against
him and his party with that remorseless virulence
which seems peculiar to priests, whether they are
persecuting or being persecuted.

After this unfortunate beginning, which tended
to the rehabilitation of the sacerdotal Gladstone,
he and his ministry did well for four years. Three
things in particular marked the dawn of a new era
in British policy. First, through the energy and
sympathy of the admirable Home Secretary,
Richard Cross, large measures of social reform were
undertaken — measures which caused Alexander
Macdonald, one of the first two Labour members
ever sent up to the House of Commons, to say in
1879 : " The Conservative party have done more
for the working classes in five years than the
Liberals have in fifty ". Some fifteen important
Acts were passed relating to such matters as
artisans' dwellings, friendly societies, trade unions,

agricultural tenancies, merchant seamen, public health, factories, enclosures, river pollution, education. The Conservatives had no such hesitation in using the power of the State to improve the condition of the people as had marked the doctrinaire politicians of the Manchester school of Liberalism. They were Collectivists in a non-Socialistic sense of the term ; that is to say, Collectivists who, while continuing to believe in the sanctity of private property, the superiority of individual enterprise, the rightness of rent for land, and the justness of interest on capital, yet held that the organised might and wisdom and wealth of the community could properly be employed to relieve poverty, redress grievances, and provide an environment for the higher life of the nation.

Secondly, in sharp contrast to the " Little Englandism " of Granville, much thought was given to the fostering and federation of the Empire. Lord Carnavon at the Colonial Office had large schemes of Imperial consolidation. Disraeli himself, with a quick imagination that instinctively responded to the call of the East, was specially concerned with the linking of Britain with the great dependency of India. It had fallen to his lot in one of the brief periods of his early office (1858) to transfer the government of India from the Company to the Crown. It was now his work, in the plenitude of his power, to secure the sea-

communication between Europe and Asia by the
purchase of the Khedive's shares in the Suez Canal
(1875) ; to flatter the pride and vivify the loyalty
of the princes and peoples of India by organising the visit of the Prince of Wales (1875) ; and,
above all, to symbolise and celebrate the permanent
union of Orient and Occident by conferring upon
the Queen the imperial crown of India (1876).

Thirdly, the prestige of Britain was revived on
the Continent, and the right of Britain to have
voice and vote in the determination of international concerns was vindicated in a way unknown
since Palmerston's day, and with a skill and tact
which perhaps no one since Wolsey had shown in
such consummate perfection. The first sign that
a new spirit had come into the conduct of foreign
affairs since the deplorable days of Granville, came
in 1875, when Germany, astonished and disquieted
by the remarkable revival of France after the
great *débâcle* of 1870–71, seemed determined to
pick a new quarrel and to complete the work of
destruction. It is as certain as anything can be
in the world of politics that if Granville had still
been at the Foreign Office nothing would have been
done to save France from extinction. Disraeli,
however, was not prepared to see the balance of
power so fatally overset. He found that Russia
viewed the prospect of the elimination of France
from the European system with equal alarm.

Between them they were able to bring so much
pressure to bear upon Berlin that the threatened
invasion of France did not take place. They did
it, too, in such a way as to elicit the formal thanks
of Bismarck ! That was where Disraeli surpassed
Palmerston.

A much more protracted and serious business
was the Near Eastern crisis of 1876–78, which
culminated in the Russo-Turkish War and the
Treaty of Berlin. Into the intricacies of the
questions at issue it is, of course, impossible to
enter here. Suffice it to say that as Disraeli
envisaged the crisis its outstanding feature was
Russia's resolve to disintegrate Turkey, secure
Constantinople, and establish a big Bulgaria completely under Russian control. He saw in this
resolve a menace to British power in the Mediterranean, and a peril to the British Empire in the
East. He was therefore determined to frustrate
Russia's designs—by diplomatic means if possible,
but if necessary even at the risk of war. Taking
his stand on the treaties of 1856 and 1871 he claimed
for Britain, as for the other signatories of those
instruments, a voice in the settlement of the
Eastern question. Defying Gladstone, who raged
against the Turk ; imposing his will upon his
dissentient colleagues, among whom seven different
policies were mooted ; resisting the importunities
of the Queen, who raged against the Russians and

threatened abdication if she could not have war ;
dominating the diplomats, who wished to see
Britain and Moscow embroiled ; even holding his
own with the mighty Bismarck, who conceived for
him a profound respect, he moulded the Concert of
Europe to his purpose, secured and controlled the
Congress of Berlin, and emerged from it having
attained his end, and bringing back to England
" Peace with Honour ". It was an amazing achievement. In accomplishing it Disraeli—since 1876
Earl of Beaconsfield—realised the loftiest aspira-
tions of *Vivian Grey* or of *Contarini Fleming*.
Alone and on the pinnacle of power he had swayed
monarchs, ruled ministers, moved armies and
navies, dictated policies, stamped the impress of
his masterful will upon the map of the world.
Bismarck, who viewed the Eastern Question with
the indifference of the more or less " honest
broker ", as he watched his lucid and decisive
handling of the complicated business, was filled
with an intense admiration. " Der alte Jude, das
ist der Mann ", he said at the close of the Congress.
He particularly approved of the British occupation
of Cyprus. " You have done a wise thing ", he
remarked to Beaconsfield, " this is progress." He
talked to him confidentially on many important
themes. He congratulated him, for instance, on
England's freedom from Socialism : " So long as
the English are devoted to horse-racing ", he

observed, " Socialism has no chance with you ".
When Beaconsfield departed from Berlin, Bismarck
put his signed photograph, together with those of
the Princess Bismarck and the Emperor William,
in the place of supreme honour in his cabinet.

That the Treaty of Berlin was, for Beaconsfield,
a personal triumph of the most spectacular kind is
beyond question. On the other hand, it is a much
controverted point whether or not the policy which
he pursued and the settlement which he achieved
were the wisest and best that the circumstances
permitted. Gladstone and the Liberals vehemently
objected to it from the first, on the ground that it
was too tender to the Turk, and too little regardful
of the interests of the Christian peoples of the
Balkans. Even Lord Salisbury, the faithful and
able colleague and helpmeet of Beaconsfield in the
great palaver, was inclined, late in life, when the
Turk had proved to be incorrigible, to fear that we
had in 1878 " put our money on the wrong horse ".
In his disgust at the perversity of the unspeakable,
he perhaps did not sufficiently realise that in the
Balkans all horses are wrong horses. The pitiful
victims of atrocities lack nothing but opportunity
in order themselves to become atrocious. That is
a truth which the painful experiences of the last
half-century have taught us. Beaconsfield knew
it in 1878, and he framed his policy accordingly.
There is much to be said in justification and defence

of this policy. It gave Eastern Europe such peace as alone seems possible for thirty-six years; it stopped the menacing advance of Russia towards the Levant, and safeguarded the communications of the British Empire; it prevented the formation of a new Holy Alliance of the autocratic empires hostile to the free peoples of the world; it rendered the subsequent development of Bulgaria harmless and therefore stable. Hence the tendency in modern criticism is to regard the Berlin settlement more favourably than was the tendency of the criticism of the intermediate generation. The difficulties of the problem are more fully recognised —the flat impossibility of doing anything except make a choice between varying degrees of badness.

The two years following the Berlin triumph (1878–80) were years of misfortune and distress. The country became involved, through the action of local officials, in unnecessary and disastrous wars in Afghanistan and Zululand; commercial depression set in; the long-deferred agricultural decline (predicted in 1846) began, and made rapid headway; nothing seemed to go well with the country or the Government. In the circumstances Gladstone's " Midlothian campaign " carried the electorate by storm, and in 1880 the ministry of Lord Beaconsfield was driven from power.

VII

Lord Beaconsfield survived his fall from power for exactly one year (April 19, 1880–April 19, 1881). During that brief period, in spite of increasing ill-health, he continued to lead his party in the House of Lords, and to pay occasional visits to the scene of his earlier labours, the House of Commons. But he realised that his life's work was done, and he gave himself more and more to meditation upon the past, and to preparation for the future which lay beyond the limits of earthly ambitions. He took out from a long-locked drawer the unfinished manuscript of a novel intended to sketch the course of British politics from the time of Canning to his own accession to office. He completed it and published it under the title *Endymion* (1880). It is the maturest, mellowest, wisest of his works. He actually began a new novel whose central figure, Joseph Toplady Falconet, was modelled upon his own life-long rival and enemy, Mr. Gladstone. Only a few chapters were ever written; but, though few, they are inimitable and sufficient; they present in unmistakable outline the full-length picture of the perfect prig. Disraeli, with all his penetration, could not understand Gladstone, any more than Gladstone, with all his piety, could forgive Disraeli. Gladstone was emotional and confused in mind; Disraeli was clear in intellect and superbly self-controlled. Gladstone was a crowd-interpreter; Disraeli a crowd-compeller. Gladstone was a man of enormous talent; Disraeli one of incontestable genius. Gladstone was an opportunist; Disraeli an idealist. Gladstone was highly ecclesiastical; Disraeli deeply religious. Gladstone's horizon was small and easily visible to the naked eye; Disraeli lived in a universe of wide expanses and large vistas. In every way they were antipathetic, contradictory, and incompatible.

Nevertheless, after Disraeli's death, Gladstone so far surmounted his ancient animosity as to pay a noble tribute to his fallen foe: " The career of Lord Beaconsfield ", he said, " is in many respects the most remarkable in our parliamentary history. For my own part I know but one that can fairly be compared to it in regard to the emotion of surprise, and, when viewed as a whole, the emotion I might almost say of wonder, which it is calculated to excite; and that is the career, and especially the earlier career, of Mr. Pitt." In the House of Lords, the Marquis of Salisbury's words of eulogy were naturally even more sympathetic and appreciative: " Zeal for the greatness of England ", he declared, " was the passion of his life ".

Three years after his death the institution of the Primrose League testified to the vitality of his ideas and the enduring vigour of his influence. The tributes which still are paid every spring, as

P

the memorable nineteenth of April recurs, bear
eloquent witness that Disraeli, as no Prime Minister
before or since has ever done, excited the interest
of the nation, quickened their imagination, fired
their ambition, and inspired their affection.

VIII

What were the principles which actuated this
strange and dazzling career ?   Concerning no Prime
Minister has the question been asked more per-
sistently ; concerning none have more divergent
answers been given. To no small extent Disraeli
was himself responsible for the mystery which
enveloped his motives and his motions. While
strongly asserting his changelessness and his consistency, he was singularly careless of appearances,
and supremely indifferent to superficial disharmonies.
He rarely troubled to explain ambiguous utterances ; he seldom thought it worth while to defend
himself against even the most malignant attacks.
In respect of the buzzing critics around him, he

> Seemed the Orient Spirit incarnate, lost
> In contemplation of the Western Soul :
>
> .   .   .   .   .
>
> Reposeful, patient, undemonstrative,
>
> .   .   .   .   .
>
> Aloof from our mutations and unrest,
> Alien to our achievements and desires,
>
> .   .   .   .   .

Another brain dreaming another dream,
Another heart recalling other loves ;

.   .   .   .   .   .

And in majestic taciturnity
Refraining his illimitable scorn.[1]

It would, indeed, have been difficult for him to make clear to the average party politician the causes which led him, without any change of ground, but with merely change of attitude, to advocate such measures as the ballot and triennial parliaments in 1832, and to oppose them in 1835; to defend Free Trade as a Tory instrument in 1841, and to condemn it as a Radical nostrum in 1846. All such things, as a matter of fact, he regarded as comparatively unimportant; they were mere means to ends, questions of expediency and not of fundamental principle. His principles had relation to concerns immeasurably more profound than devices of government or modes of commercial regulation.

Not unnaturally, however, his enemies—the Whigs and their allies—concentrating their attention upon his apparent tergiversations, roundly accused him of being an unprincipled adventurer. This, indeed, is the inspiring theme of Mr. Thomas Macknight's *Literary and Political Biography*.[2] Still more prominent is it in the terrific tirade which Mr. T. P. O'Connor in his fiery youth launched against the great opponent of Home Rule, under

---

[1] William Watson, *A Study in Contrasts.*
[2] Note specially pp. 280 and 489.

the title *Lord Beaconsfield, a Biography* (1878). He describes his victim as " an unscrupulous and unprincipled cynic " ; asserts that " throughout his whole career his sole absorbing thought has been *himself* ", and " that to carry out his own advancement he has sacrificed every principle which men hold dear ". He compares him to Vivian Grey, the hero of the juvenile novel of 1826, and endeavours in enormous detail to prove that " Lord Beaconsfield's character is essentially a counterpart of that of Vivian Grey " and that " Lord Beaconsfield's political career has been conducted upon the same arts as were practised by the hero of his earliest story ".

Both these so-called " biographies " were written during the heat and tumult of embittered party conflict. As lapse of time led the political hurlyburly away to other fields, and concentrated the struggle round other leaders, later investigators were able at greater leisure and with less passion to study afresh the words and deeds of Disraeli in the endeavour to discover the mainsprings of his life. Froude's short biography (1900) was the first serious attempt at an impartial survey. It swept away as absurd all the extreme accusations of its predecessors : " In public or private ", it concluded, " he had never done a dishonourable action ; he had disarmed hatred and never lost a personal friend ". The supreme and final vindication, however, had to be reserved for the great six-volumed life, published 1910–20, by Messrs. Monypenny and Buckle. There, on the basis of all the evidence, the judgment is given : " There is no lack of the deep consistency which has its roots in a highly original mind, and in a strong intellectual grasp of certain cardinal ideas ; in a temperament of a marked idiosyncrasy, and in a character of exceptional persistence ". This view is supported by Dr. Wingfield-Stratford in his excellent *History of English Patriotism* (1913). " Never ", he says, " did Statesman make so little concealment of his principles ; never was action so firmly, so inevitably based upon them." And again, " His mind was always expanding, but the main principles of his philosophy were knit together by bonds stronger than adamant, and he never shuffled or shifted his ground ".

From what sources do we derive our knowledge of these fundamental and determining principles of Disraeli's career ? First, we have his multitudinous speeches in Parliament, as recorded in Hansard ; and his rare but highly important orations to public audiences, as reported in the newspaper press. Secondly, there are the numerous articles which, especially in his earlier days, whether under his own name or under some pseudonym, he contributed to such organs as the *Times*, the *Morning Post*, or (his own creation) the *Press* (1855–59).

Thirdly, we can turn to his formal political writings published in book form, and especially to the *Vindication of the English Constitution* (1835) ; the *Letters of Runnymede* (1836) ; and the *Lord George Bentinck : a Political Biography* (1851). Next, thanks to Messrs. Monypenny and Buckle, we can now draw upon the inexhaustible treasure-house of his private letters and papers incorporated in their great biography. But finally—and still most important of all—we have the priceless heritage of the novels. In these, more than in any other source, is the real Disraeli revealed. Here, under the thin disguise of fiction, he poured forth his own deep sentiments and displayed his brilliant ideas. All his novels are autobiographical ; all deal with young men aspiring to political power ; all depict some aspect of his own complex character and varied experience. He had a lively imagination, but it was analytical, not synthetic ; interpretive, not creative. It needed concrete character and substantive events to work on. Hence Disraeli is always his own hero : Vivian Grey, the young Duke, Contarini Fleming, Alroy, Coningsby, Egremont (in *Sybil*), Tancred, Lothair, Endymion ; all are embodiments of some aspect of himself. Similarly, the secondary characters in the novels are mainly representations of his own contemporaries, and representations so true to life as to be recognisable with embarrassing facility. In respect of

Vivian Grey, identification tables containing over fifty names were printed and sold for the edification of such of the middle class as wished to conceal their unfamiliarity with the aristocratic world and its parasites.

Such, then, are the sources of our knowledge of Disraeli's ideas and principles. What were the sources from which he derived those ideas and principles themselves ? To some extent he was influenced by the writers and thinkers of his own day—by, *e.g.*, Cobbett, Carlyle, Coleridge, Southey, Byron, Shelley. Still more was he moulded by his studies of the statesmen of the older days—in particular, Canning, Pitt, Shelburne, Chatham, Wyndham ; of all of whom he has left penetrating and appreciative accounts. But two men, above all others, were his inspirers and his guides. These two were Bolingbroke and Burke—Bolingbroke in his earlier days, Burke in his later days. From Bolingbroke he learned his primitive hatred of the Whigs, his patriotic devotion to England, his reverence for monarchy. From Burke he learned the deeper lessons of respect for religion as the indispensable basis for stable society ; regard for tradition as the veritable life-giving spirit of a people ; recognition of the need of constant reform as a means of keeping the organic State in healthy correspondence with its environment ; acceptance of the party system as a necessary instrument of

parliamentary government. In so far as Disraeli
developed as a political idealist during the course
of his career, his development was a movement
from Bolingbroke to Burke. It is well known that
Burke, if his days had not been cut prematurely
short, would, at the end of the eighteenth century,
have taken his seat in the House of Lords as " Earl
of Beaconsfield ". Is it too much to suppose that
Disraeli in assuming this title in 1876 indicated
his homage to the great master to whom he owed
so many of his conceptions ?

I wonder if any one ever told Disraeli, towards
the end of his life, that he had become a Whig ?
If so, that may account for the expression of profound melancholy which marks all his later portraits.
For he must have realised that it was the truth.
In no essential did his later creed differ from that
of Palmerston, or Hartington, or Rosebery, or
indeed any other sensible person.

IX

I have spoken of Disraeli's " ideas and principles ". The two must be kept distinct from one
another. Principles, it is true, imply ideas ; but
they are more than ideas. They are *operative*
ideas ; ideas in action ; intellectual conceptions
applied continuously and consistently to practical
affairs ; thoughts impelled by emotion, will, and

even conscience. Ideas may be infinite in number :
principles are necessarily few ; perhaps, in the last
analysis, they may, in each individual case, be
reduced to a single one.

Disraeli was rich in ideas. They were generated
freely in his luxuriant and imaginative mind. They
flowed from him in a copious and constant stream,
like light from radium—ideas original and arrest-
ing ; some indeed fantastic, others profound. Mr.
John Bailey, speaking of the second section of Mr.
Monypenny's biography, which covers the years
1837–46, says, " In the novels and speeches dealt
with in this volume alone there is more matter for
political thought than in all the utterances of all
the other English statesmen of the nineteenth
century put together ". This is a remarkable
judgment ; but if I hesitate to endorse it, I do
so merely because I have not yet succeeded in
examining " all the utterances of all the other
English statesmen of the nineteenth century ".

It would be a colossal though eminently re-
munerative task to collect and classify the audacious
and original ideas which sparkle in all Disraeli's
writings and in many of his speeches. That task,
however, cannot be attempted here. It must
suffice to mention that among the most prominent
are his exalted conception of race as the dominant
factor in history ; his emphasis on the influence of
personality as the prime determinant of the course

of affairs ; his curious view of Christianity as merely
" completed Judaism " and therefore of Judaism
as essential Christianity — whence his remarkable
definition of the Church as " a sacred corporation for
the promotion and maintenance in Europe of certain
Asian principles " ; his highly novel and peculiar
opinions respecting the course of English history
and the nature of the English Constitution. No
one can read his works or peruse the reports of his
spoken utterances without realising that one is in
the presence of a powerful and independent mind,
distinctly Oriental in its outlook, and singularly
free from the prejudices and prepossessions that
commonly characterise the denizens of Great
Britain.

We turn from his ideas to his principles, that is
to say, to the deep underlying conceptions which
were the foundations of his policy and the motives
of his actions. They are, as we have already
remarked, strikingly reminiscent of those of Burke.
They can be grouped under four main heads, as
follows : first, the religious basis of society ;
secondly, the organic nature of the State ; thirdly,
the solidarity of the community ; fourthly, the
need for the maintenance of a balance of power
and interests in the body social, economic, and
politic.

1. *The Religious Basis of Society.*—Disraeli was
profoundly religious, as every one will realise who

has carefully and sympathetically studied his three novels, *Alroy*, *Tancred*, and *Lothair*, to say nothing of his other works wherein the divine motive is less prominent. His religion was not, of course, that of Gladstone, nor that of Bright, nor even that of the majority of his own associates. It was something of an " Asian mystery " ; something of that elusive cult referred to in *Endymion*, the secret of whose nature " sensible men never tell ". It was a religion, however, which included a profound and permeating faith in the reality of the providential government of the world, and the divine superintendence of human affairs. It was a religion whose specific creed was doubtful; but this at least was evident, that it looked not to Canterbury, or to Rome, or to Byzantium, but to Jerusalem as its centre and most holy place. The Church of England was regarded by Disraeli as a national institution, and only as such did he view it with enthusiasm. He respected it as a form of completed Judaism adapted to the English climate by means of a number of Acts of Parliament and judicial decisions of the Privy Council. He, therefore, resisted Ritualists who would de-nationalise and Romanise it ; Rationalists who would naturalise and Germanise it; Liberationists who would disestablish and disendow it. He held that in a unique and inimitable manner it reconciled authority and freedom; orthodoxy and toleration; the

State recognition of religion with a wide and wise allowance of private prophesying.

2. *The Organic Nature of the State.*—He looked upon the State not as a mechanical contrivance based on convention or contract, owing its construction to a perception of utility ; but rather as something akin to an organisation, containing a principle of life, subject to laws of growth, liable to injury, decay, and death. Hence he emphasised, on the one hand, the idea of continuity — the principle of order — which exalted immemorial tradition, long-prevalent custom, and established law. On the other hand, he stressed the idea of adaptation to environment—the principle of progress—which held perpetually prominent the need of constant reform in order to keep ancient institutions in harmony with new wants and new conditions.

3. *The Solidarity of the Community.*—In clear, and probably conscious, opposition to Karl Marx, he repudiated the conception of " class war ", and proclaimed the unity of the nation. In particular, he maintained that the Tory party was " national or nothing ". He contrasted it both with the Communists who formed a proletarian sect, and the Liberals who boasted an anti-patriotic cosmopolitanism. This idea of the solidarity of the community had for him many and important practical implications. It lay at the base of his

defence of the Corn Laws: he called upon all ranks and orders of society to consent, if necessary, to pay more for their bread in order to prevent the agricultural interest from suffering extinction. It was the source of his advocacy of factory laws, public health acts, housing regulations, and social reform generally. He had no hesitation in using the power of the State in the interest of the community as a whole, or of any menaced portion of it. He was profoundly convinced that if any one member were injured, all the body politic would suffer loss.

4. *Need of Balance of Powers and Interests.*— Disraeli's was a markedly moderate mind. It recoiled instinctively from extremes. More and more as his ideas shaped themselves into a system did he envisage a constitution in which innumerable groups and varied interests would move in equipoised harmony, like planets in a constellation. He strove to secure a balance of classes in society; a balance of factors in economics; a balance of estates in the constitution; a balance of orders in the electorate; a balance between local and central government; a balance between the mother country and the dominions in the empire; a balance between the British Empire and the other great States in the Commonwealth of the World.

X

It would take us too much into detail to trace the particular lines of policy which Disraeli's principles led him to pursue. They may, however, be epitomised in the four words, conservatism, collectivism, patriotism, and imperialism.

First, his *conservatism* caused him to bend all his endeavours to preserve the constitution of both State and Church. He strove to exalt the power and prestige of the monarchy; to defend the prescriptive rights of the House of Lords; to prevent the character of the House of Commons from being destroyed by radical " reforms "; to save the Established Church from its subverters; to safeguard the territorial bases of the English system of administration.

Secondly, his *collectivism* led him, as we have already observed, to employ all the resources of the State for social ends. That element, and that alone, the conservative collectivism of Disraeli had with the socialistic collectivism of the Fabian Society, which was inaugurated within a few years of his death. Collectivism is merely a means to an end, and the conservative end is poles apart from the socialistic end. The collectivism of the Fabians aims at the suppression of private enterprise, the abolition of rent paid to landlords, and the elimination of interest paid to capitalists. On

the other hand, the collectivism of Disraeli aims at
the provision of the conditions of a better social
life, precisely in order that private enterprise may
be less fettered, in order that higher rents may be
payable out of a greater prosperity, and in order
that capital may abound, yielding a threefold
increase. To Disraeli personality was the key to
progress. He had no faith in " the inevitability of
gradualness ", or in the gradualness of inevitability,
or in economic determinism, or in any other specious
phrase which concealed the desire of the inefficient
many to live at the expense of the energetic few.

Thirdly, his *patriotism* compelled him to regard
the safeguarding of British interests and the maintenance of British prestige as the prime duty of a
British minister. It has been said that no statesman in this country since Wolsey, ever surveyed
the world of foreign affairs with so wide and com-
prehensive a gaze as did Disraeli. The fact that
he had no drop of British blood in his veins; the
fact that his family had been in England no more
than fifty-six years when he was born ; the fact
that his alien origin and his Jewish faith kept him
during his early years aloof from the current of
English social and political life, gave him a
singular detachment in his contemplation of the
problems of diplomacy. But beyond most of his
" all-British " colleagues, and far more than his
cosmopolitan opponents—such as Cobden, Bright,

and Gladstone—he investigated them for the purpose of discovering how they might be solved in such a manner as to increase the wealth, the honour, and the glory of the land which he had made his own, and to which he had become attached with a passionate devotion.

Finally, his *imperialism* was the fruit of his recognition of the limitless possibilities which lay in the vast and scattered dominions and dependencies constituting the British Empire. He was not eager for further expansion, and if he secured control over such an island as Cyprus, he did so in order to guard the communications of Britain with regions already possessed. What he greatly desired was its unification and consolidation, so that it might as a single and undivided whole take its fitting place in the world of great empires—German, Russian, French, American — which was taking shape visibly before the eyes of the men of his day.

XI

Although this essay has already reached its allotted limits, it is impossible to conclude it without some attempt to estimate the character, assess the ability, summarise the achievement, and indicate the influence of the great man whose principles have been under review.

His character seems to me to have been compounded of four great groups of qualities; but above and beyond these there was an element of subtlety, complexity, mystery, individuality that defies all analysis. " Nature ", he once remarked, " has given me an awful ambition ", and first among his characteristics must be placed his passion for prominence and power. He was conscious of the possession of vast abilities ; he had an immense capacity for command ; he longed with an insatiable desire for leadership ; he was uneasy in any subordinate place, where his dynamic originality could not have full scope. Closely akin to his ambition was, secondly, his lordly self-confidence and amazing courage. He was afflicted by no hesitations ; he laboured under no apprehensions ; he feared no foe, rather he singled out the greatest and most formidable as the only enemies worthy of his attack. He formed his own opinions, careless whether he was in a minority or a majority. He expressed his opinion, however unpopular, with unflinching clarity : no man who was a self-seeking adventurer merely out for office would have spoken for the Chartists as he did ; have voted in a minority of three against the Birmingham police ; have attacked the Maynooth grant against, not only Peel, but also his " Young England " friends ; or have advocated the admission of Jews to Parliament on grounds which offended the sentiments of both the supporters and the opponents of that measure. No one who thought primarily of place in a Conservative party would have written *Sybil*, with its scathing exposures of both the territorial and the commercial nobility. No one who wished above all to conciliate hostile prejudices would have published to the world the religion of *Tancred*. He wanted to lead—he was determined to lead—the Tory party ; but it would have to be a Tory party created, educated, and inspired by himself alone.

That he achieved his purpose was due, thirdly, to his possession in an unusual degree of a patience which no delays could out-tire ; a fortitude which no rebuffs could daunt ; an equanimity which no animosities could ruffle ; a magnanimity which no malice could destroy. The way in which for a quarter of a century (1849–1874) he led his people through the wilderness, beating off attacks, calming revolts, healing schisms, allaying jealousies, removing dislikes, mitigating suspicions, winning confidence, devotion, and affection—the way in which he did all this is a miracle of forbearance and endurance. Contrast the behaviour and the fate of Lord Randolph Churchill, who in the next generation had to deal with much the same situation as that in which Disraeli attained his ultimate triumph. This study in contrasts should suggest the fourth group of qualities in which Disraeli excelled, viz. tact, geniality, bonhomie, power of avoiding offence, soothing vanity, conciliating hostility, gaining love. The interested will find it a fascinating quest to trace the process by which he won the confidence and regard of four great people who, all of them, at one time or another, distrusted and disliked him—Lord Derby, Lord Salisbury, the Prince Consort, Queen Victoria. They will not complete their inquiry without an enhanced respect for all the persons concerned.

Of Disraeli's abilities it is needless further to speak. His was a nature singularly well-balanced and complete. His powers of intellect—his grasp, insight, alertness, wit—were combined with an unusual strength of will and a profound depth of emotion. Few, if any, in Parliament have equalled him in debate; in quickness in seeing his opponent's point; in effectiveness in parrying and turning it. Few in office have excelled him in resolution or persistence of purpose. The carrying of the Reform Act of 1867 and the conclusion of the Treaty of Berlin in 1878 are the two outstanding monuments of his masterful personality in politics.

These two things rank as his most conspicuous isolated achievements. But more important than they, were the results of his long and patient leadership, viz. the reconstruction of the Tory party after its ruin in 1846; the education of the Tory party away from protection and into reform; the conversion of the Tory party from a class

confederacy into a national organisation ; the discovery of the Tory working-man ; the creation of
the Tory democracy. Says Dr. Wingfield-Stratford : " He weaned the great party of which he
was a member from a selfish opportunism to a
noble trust in the people. He bequeathed three
cardinal principles for its guidance—social reform,
imperialism, and the maintenance of our constitution. He broke decisively with the tradition of
shirking responsibility and governing by a tradesman's calculation of profit and loss. Above all,
he opened the souls of Englishmen to the consciousness of a free empire, a calling and a dignity not
inferior to that of Rome." [1]

Thus it is that while the influence of most
Victorian prime ministers has become faint and
indistinguishable, and while the memory of the
majority has grown dim, the influence of Disraeli
is still living and operative, and his memory a
flowering evergreen.

[1] *History of English Patriotism*, ii. 585.

Photo. Lyddel Sawyer.

WILLIAM EWART GLADSTONE

MR. W. E. GLADSTONE

By Ramsay Muir

I

Nobody would deny to Gladstone a place in any list, however short, of the great representative figures of the nineteenth century. For nearly half a century he stood forth, in the eyes not of Englishmen alone but of all Europe, as almost the personification of the Liberal idea, just as Bismarck embodied the authoritarian idea. There was, indeed, a remarkable parallelism between the lives of these two great men. Both were born under the shadow of the Napoleonic War—Gladstone in 1809, when Napoleon was at his apogee; Bismarck in 1815, the moment of his fall. Both emerged into European celebrity at almost the same moment, about 1850, when the revolutionary period was at an end, and the states of Europe were setting to work to determine the principles by which they meant their development to be controlled. Both achieved supreme power at about the same time, in the 'sixties, the one as the leader

of a democratic, the other as the leader of a mon-
archic and militarist movement. And after stormy
careers in which both inspired a degree of devotion
and of hatred such as few other statesmen have
aroused, both ended their public careers with the
feeling that they were swept aside by new movements with which they were out of sympathy.
Both died in the same year, 1898, having become in
their own lifetimes almost legendary figures, whose
disappearance seemed to, and indeed did, mark the
end of an era. In the eyes of the world one stood
for liberty, the other for authority ; one for persuasion, the other for force, as the ultimate determinant in human affairs ; one for individual
freedom and distrust of State action, the other
for the complete subordination of the individual
to the State. There could not be a more pointed
contrast. These two great men in truth personi-
fied two rival tendencies which had been at work
in European politics throughout the century, and
which came to a final and desperate clash in the
Great War.

Happily I am not required to deal with Gladstone's full and varied career, and its astonishing
changes. My task is only to discuss his political
principles. But this in itself is difficult enough,
because his principles were gradually developed in
the course of a remarkable intellectual pilgrimage.
They were, in truth, the outcome of the interplay

of his powerful mind and character with the series
of events with which he had to deal. It may fairly
be said of Gladstone that there have been few
statesmen of his eminence and intellectual accomplishment who have been so loth to formulate or
to act upon a definite political theory. He was
no doctrinaire ; he had no theory of the kind of
society he wished to shape by political action. His
business throughout life, as he himself put it, was
" to work the institutions of his country ". He
never defined beforehand the changes he wished
to achieve ; it was only when some problem that
demanded solution forced itself upon his attention
that he set himself to work it out. " I have not
been so happy ", he himself said, " at any time of
my life, as to be able sufficiently to adjust the
proper conditions of handling any difficult question,
until the question itself was at the door ". And
this does not mean merely that he did not work
out the detail of his solution until the question
became urgent ; it means that he did not think
seriously about the question at all. A very shrewd
and friendly observer—Mr. Meredith Townshend
of the *Spectator*—said of him in 1864, when he was
on the eve of his most striking period of achievement, " Mr. Gladstone has done less to lay down
any systematised course of action than almost any
man of his political standing ". This is not only
a true and a sound observation ; it is a guide to

much that would otherwise be bewildering in his
political development. He was essentially an em-
piric, docile to the teachings of experience. He did
not start with a set of fixed ideas or formulæ about
the constitution of society, and strive to bring them
to realisation : he was the pupil, though not the
creature, of events, and his political ideas were
shaped by experience working upon a character
and an intellect of extraordinary native force.

II

Following this clue, we shall best be able to
appreciate the Gladstonian ideas in politics if we
first get some grasp of the kind of man he was, and
then observe the impact upon him of experience
in one sphere after another. I despair of doing
justice, in a few sentences, to a personality so
potent and so full of paradox ; but there are some
things about him so undeniable that there is no
difficulty in setting them down. To begin with,
Nature had been lavish to him in physical and
mental gifts. He had a frame of steel, a presence
that commanded respect, an eye of an extraordinarily piercing power, a voice of infinite richness
and charm. Without these physical gifts he could
not have borne the incessant labours which he
undertook : even in extreme old age, his endurance
and resilience, his power to answer to every call,

amazed and dazzled those who came in contact with him.

His native intellectual endowments were no less remarkable, and he reinforced them with an untiring industry, an extraordinary gift of concentration, and a capacity to utilise every flying minute, which can never have been surpassed. Even as a boy at school, his range of reading was astounding ; his diaried notes of the books he found time to read even when the pressure of public business was at its height fill one with despair ; and from boyhood till his last days this devouring energy in the acquisition of knowledge continued without relaxation. One is sometimes inclined to wonder whether he would not have been a yet greater man if he had sometimes allowed himself to be idle, to ruminate, to chew the cud of thought, to let the flood of knowledge which he was constantly assimilating soak more quietly into the recesses of his mind.

To all this he added an unequalled facility and copiousness of expression in speech and writing — far too great a facility, indeed. Without it, no doubt, he could not have exercised the dominating power which he wielded, but if he had spoken and written less easily, we should have remembered more of what he said and wrote. It was this boundless fluency of expression, combined with his congenital unwillingness to commit himself to definite opinions until he was faced by a definite issue, which led him into that involved and highly qualified form of statement that caused so many to mistrust him.

He had, in an unequalled degree, the temperament of the orator—the gift of passionate belief in the importance of the issue with which he was dealing, the born fighter's unwillingness to yield any point to an opponent, and an instinctive power of feeling the sense of his audience and adjusting himself to it without modifying his convictions. This was, no doubt, a temptation to him : he was apt to " think in speeches ", towards persuasion rather than towards the discovery of truth. But he was saved from the dangers of this temperament by the fundamental qualities of his character. With all his masterful power, he was a modest man, if it be modesty to measure oneself always against the ideal rather than against one's competitors. With all his subtlety and finesse of intellect, he was a simple man : Jowett said of him, when he became Prime Minister, " It is the first time that any one of such simplicity has been in so exalted a station ". With all his caution, he was a man of infinite courage : once he had made up his mind upon the rightness of a course of action, nothing could deflect him, least of all any consideration of self-interest.

At the root of all this, the very foundation of his character, the impregnable rock upon which he stood, was his profound religious belief. All

his life through, amid his immense labours, he was
borne up by an absolute confidence that he was
serving God, and that God was with him.   There
was in this belief no self-righteousness, no assertion
of personal inspiration.   He did not obtrude it in
public business or in private relations ; he was
able to combine it with a noble and widening
tolerance which never qualified his own certainty ;
and the agnostic Morley, who was the chosen con-
fidant of his later years, records that Gladstone
never once distressed him with religious discussions in all their intercourse.   But if he did not
obtrude his belief, neither did he conceal it.   It
was the staff of his life ; and in his brief diary
jottings, which recorded, in the baldest shorthand,
speeches, interviews, social engagements, and books
read, there continually recur brief quiet references
to the source from which, as he believed, he drew
his strength.   This was the ultimate secret of his
power to go on with his incessant labours whether
the skies were dark or bright.   This was the secret,
also, of the loyalty, almost approaching to adora-
tion, which he inspired in thousands of simple folk.
" You do not know how those of us regard you ",
Spurgeon wrote to him in 1882, " who feel it a joy
to live when a premier believes in righteousness.
We believe in no man's infallibility, but it is restful
to be sure of one man's integrity."   Finally it was
this which gave unity to his amazing pilgrimage of

opinion, and which ballasted a noble ship that lacked the anchorage of fixed and clearly defined political theories.

III

This powerful and masculine personality began his life in an atmosphere of rigid conservatism. His earliest political passion was stirred by opposition to the Reform Act of 1832. His deepest concern was the maintenance of the religious character of the State, which, as he then believed, involved the exclusion from many privileges of Dissenters, Catholics, and Free-thinkers. He entered Parliament as the nominee of the Duke of Newcastle for what was, even in 1832, the practically pocket borough of Newark, and he expressed the utmost deference for his patron, whose political authority seemed to him to be rooted in the natural order of things. His first speeches were made in the defence of the slave-system whereby his father's estates in Demerara were worked.

But in one sphere after another, as he was brought up against facts, his conscience and his intellect drove him to a solution violently in conflict with his traditions; and his courage forced him to accept the teachings of his conscience, at whatever cost to himself. He never underwent a wholesale conversion: he passed from Toryism to Liberalism by stages; and there were some spheres in which he never made the change at all. "It has been experience which has altered my politics" he himself wrote in 1880, after his violent breach with accepted traditions on the Eastern question. "My Toryism was accepted by me on authority and in good faith ; I did my best to fight for it. But . . . on every subject, as I came to deal with it practically, I *had* to deal with it as a Liberal." Or, again, " I was brought up to distrust and dislike liberty, I learned to believe in it. That is the key to all my changes."

The change began where one would expect it, in that sphere which meant most to him, the sphere of religion. During the 'thirties, after leaving Oxford, he passed from the evangelical doctrine in which he was bred to the High-Church view of Pusey and the Tractarians. This movement of religious thought in his own mind was a thing so momentous to him that it modified his whole outlook. The religious life meant so much for him that it seemed horrible to restrict by authority the religious life of others. Not without pain, he came to the conclusion, soon after the publication of his book on *Church and State*, that the authoritative enforcement of a State religion was at once impracticable and unjust in the modern State. So it came to pass that the High Churchman, without wavering in his own beliefs, came to be an advocate of the removal of Jewish disabilities, and of the admission of Dissenters to the universities, the noblest and most moving defender of the right of the atheist Bradlaugh to take his place in Parliament, and the disestablisher of the Church in Ireland. It was about 1850—in many ways a turning-point in his career—that this complete acceptance of liberty of conscience became a central part of his creed. " Here once for all," he said (speaking on the Vatican decrees in 1851), " I enter my most solemn, earnest and deliberate protest against all attempts to meet the spiritual dangers of our Church by temporal legislation of a penal character." At that date he still regarded himself as a Conservative. Nor was it only a consideration of practical wisdom which had led him to this conclusion. His new-formed tolerance had deeper roots. " I have no mental difficulty ", he wrote about this time, " in reconciling a belief in the Church . . . with the comforting persuasion that those who do not receive this greatest blessing . . . are, notwithstanding, the partakers, each in his measure, of other gifts, and will be treated according to their use of them . . . I was brought up to think otherwise. . . . But long, long, have I cast these weeds behind me." And this profound change of view was insensibly affecting his whole outlook, and making him ready for other changes. In 1851, in a published letter to a Scottish prelate on Church affairs, he wrote, " I am deeply convinced that all systems, *whether religious or political*, which rest on a principle of absolutism, must of necessity be feeble and ineffective systems ; and that methodically to enlist the members of a community in the performance of its public duties is the way to make that community powerful and healthful ".

IV

The next stage in this pilgrimage of opinion may be dated from the moment when Sir Robert Peel, to his immense surprise, put him into what seemed the highly inappropriate office of the Board of Trade, and employed him as his right-hand man in the immense work of tariff readjustment which ended in the Repeal of the Corn Laws. The appointment was a stroke of genius.   Till then, engrossed in Church matters, Gladstone had taken no interest in trade or finance ; and he had been a hard-shell protectionist, regarding the protective system as part of the accepted social organisation. But once his devouring energy and industry were turned upon economic problems, he underwent a rapid, complete, and lasting conversion. He became a more convinced and uncompromising Free Trader than Peel himself, and the doctrine of Free Trade became one of his main political anchors. In this sphere he was to display his genius most impressively — so impressively that it came to be assumed that his supreme gifts lay in finance. His great budgets laid down the principles of British finance, and established the sleepless treasury watchfulness and the rigid economy which marked our financial system until a recent date. Gladstone whole-heartedly accepted the principle that wealth fructifies best when it is left in the pockets of the citizen. These ideas brought him very near in sympathy to the Manchester school, and first Cobden and then Bright became his nearest associates and warmest supporters. But, being never a doctrinaire, Gladstone never identified himself completely with the Manchester school. Late in life he indignantly repudiated the idea that the Liberal party, under his leadership, had ever accepted the pure individualist doctrine of *laissez-faire*. Indeed, Townshend of the *Spectator* noted of him in 1864 that " he does not hesitate to apply the full powers of the State to ameliorate social anomalies, as he showed by creating State banks, State insurance offices, and State annuities for the very poor ". So far was he from being a doctrinaire individualist that in 1844, when at the Board of Trade, he was anxious to nationalise the railways ; and although Peel was not ready for this, it was Gladstone who was responsible for the Railways Act of that year, which defined the principles of State regulation of monopolies, requiring from the railway companies a very full

publicity of accounts, and reserving for the State
the power of fixing prices, *i.e.* of fares and rates—
drastic remedies which nobody has yet had the
courage to apply to other monopolies.

V

The third field in which Gladstone found himself driven by the pressure of events out of the
traditional Tory attitude into a Liberal attitude
was the field of colonial administration. The early
part of his career formed the period in which the
new British colonial system was being established.
It had two aspects : first, the protection of the
rights of backward peoples ; second, the establishment of a system of full self-government in the
colonies of British stock. On the first head,
Gladstone dates his own conversion to the debates
on the Bill for the emancipation of slaves in 1833.
His change of attitude distressed his father. But
the quondam defender of slavery had soon " cast
these weeds behind him " ; and although, in the
later part of his career, he took no very direct
part in colonial administration, his whole support
was given to that beneficent change, inspired
largely by the missionaries, which transformed the
relation of the colonial administrator towards the
backward peoples from that of exploitation to that
of trusteeship.

R

On the second issue—the development of self-government in the colonies of British stock —this was a period of critical importance. There were two dominant schools of thought on colonial questions : the purely Tory attitude, resolute to maintain domination ; and the *laissez-aller* attitude, which regarded the colonies as mere burdens—in Disraeli's phrase, " millstones round our necks ". This school held that the colonies were certain sooner or later to claim independence, and that they ought to be enabled to do so as quickly as possible. But there was a third group, that of the Radical Imperialists, headed by Durham, Wakefield, Molesworth, and Mill, who attached a high value to the colonial connection, but held that it could best be maintained by a full participation of freedom. In this they were the inheritors of the ideals of Burke. Gladstone found himself drawn to this school of thought, and in a debate on the Australian Colonies Bill of 1850, in which even Lord John Russell frankly associated himself with the " cut-the-painter " school, Gladstone gave the best expression to the doctrine of Burke and of Durham. " Experience has proved ", he said, " that if you want to strengthen the connection between the colonies and this country, if you want to see British institutions adopted and beloved in the colonies, you must never associate with them the hated name of force and coercion adopted by

us. . . . Their natural disposition is to love and
revere the name of England, and this reverence is
by far the best security you can have for their
continuing not only to be subjects of the Crown,
but to render it that allegiance which is the most
precious of all—the allegiance which proceeds
from the depths of the heart of man." Whatever
his critics might say, Gladstone was never a Little
Englander. He had grasped the conception of the
British Commonwealth as a partnership of free
peoples.

Here, once more, at the date (1850) which I have
already described as a turning-point in Gladstone's
political development, was a proclamation of liberty
rather than authority as the cement of peoples,
which is the essence of the Liberal creed. It was
inevitable that the tone of thought here expressed
should modify the attitude towards the idea of
democracy at home of the man who had begun his
career as a vehement opponent of the Reform Act
of 1832. But, as we have remarked, Gladstone's
mind was so built that he was incapable of defining
his attitude until a problem became practically
urgent. Even during the long and vague discussions
of the late 'fifties and early 'sixties, he wrapped himself in characteristic ambiguities, the source of which
was the difficulty of reconciling an avoidance of
definite issues with the new orientation of his
thought. It was not until 1864 that he made the

famous declaration which constituted him the inevitable leader of a new Liberalism : " Every man who is not presumably incapacitated by some consideration of personal unfitness or of political danger is morally entitled to come within the pale of the constitution ". Even this famous pronouncement was, when examined closely, found to be full of reservations. But there was implied in it the same governing idea which was expressed in the 1850 letter to the Bishop of Aberdeen, and which was now the controlling idea of Gladstone's political thought—the idea of participation in the duties of citizenship as the best cement of States.

The ice of a Tory tradition melted slowly. Almost to the end of his days Gladstone retained a veneration for the hereditary principle which was strongly in conflict with any outright democratic creed ; and it was not until 1894 that he was prepared to launch an open campaign against the House of Lords. In truth, Gladstone was never a democrat in any crude or sweeping sense : he regarded the system of democracy primarily as opening the career for natural aristocrats. " You think one man is as good as another, whereas I am a believer in aristocracy," Ruskin once said to him. " Oh dear, no ! " Gladstone replied. " I am nothing of the sort. I am a firm believer in the aristocratic principle—the rule of the best. I am an out-and-out inequalitarian." Nevertheless, the declaration of 1864 was the beginning of his career as a popular leader, the like of whom no modern country had hitherto seen. It was he, the instinctive conservative, profoundly venerating the Crown and the privileges of Parliament, who was the first to go beyond Parliament in a direct appeal to the mass of the people ; and his political progresses, especially from 1878 onwards, profoundly changed the conditions of English politics. He had learnt to appeal from the politicians to the people. And the effect upon his own mind was very deep.

VI

But I am inclined to think that the field in which Gladstone's slowly maturing Liberalism was most remarkably displayed, and produced the greatest fruits, was the field of foreign policy. There is a popular belief that his highest achievements lay in the field of finance; and no doubt, in actual measurable attainment, there is nothing else in his career which equals his financial work. But if the test of greatness in a statesman is rather to be found in his influence upon the mind of his generation and upon its future course of action than in his actual achievements, I think it may fairly be claimed that foreign policy was the sphere in which Gladstone's ideas counted for most. It was in 1850—again note this significant date—that he first made an

important pronouncement which showed the new
orientation of his mind. The occasion was the
famous debate on Don Pacifico, in which all the
most powerful speakers of that day combined to
attack Palmerston's somewhat insolent and dictatorial methods. Gladstone then expressed what
it has since become fashionable to describe as a
" European " point of view: " Let us do as we
would be done by. Let us pay all the respect to a
feeble state and to the infancy of free institutions
which we should desire and exact from others
towards their authority and strength." Here was
a note far removed from the arrogant " Civis
Romanus sum " of Palmerston, and equally removed from that dictatorship of the Great Powers
which was the nineteenth-century form of internationalism. But ere long Gladstone was to find
himself on Palmerston's side, in a protest against
gross misgovernment. A visit to Naples showed
him the ugliness of Bomba's tyranny. He came
home white-hot with indignation, and in defiance
of all the counsels of prudence and international
etiquette, insisted upon publishing a glowing and
uncompromising denunciation of these iniquities
which shocked all the chanceries and made him a
hero of the Italian nationalists. Yet he was so
reluctant to commit himself to any doctrinaire
theories that he was slow to admit the Mazzinian
doctrine of nationality. But his sympathy and

anger had been aroused. On each practical issue as it arose, in the *risorgimento* struggle, his voice was heard on the nationalist side ; and the Italians were right in seeing in him one of the warmest advocates of their cause. In all this he found himself in unexpected sympathy with Palmerston, from whom he later confessed that he had learnt one of his great lessons in Liberalism ; and perhaps this alone enabled him to work in harness with Palmerston during his last ministry. This new outlook in international affairs, this gradual accept-ance of the nationalist idea, was displayed in other fields also. He denounced the obstacles placed by the Great Powers in the way of the union of the principalities into the new state of Rumania ; and, as Chief Commissioner, he was largely responsible for the cession of the Ionian Islands to Greece— perhaps the only instance of the voluntary cession of territory by a great power to a small one of which there is any record. Thus, almost in his own despite, Gladstone became, in the eyes of Europe, the great exponent of the rights of small peoples, and of the cause of national unity and freedom. He never attended a European conference ; he never shaped a great European treaty ; he never even sat in the Foreign Office. Yet during his life, and still more when he died, there came to him such tributes from the little nations as no European statesman of his time received.

The culmination of this aspect of Gladstone's development came in the Homeric contest which he waged against Disraeli on the Eastern question, from 1876 to 1880. This was, indeed, one of the greatest debates on a broad issue of principle that English politics, usually chary of such discussions, have ever seen ; and it was perhaps the most astonishing achievement of his career.

Gladstone's prestige had greatly dwindled at the close of his ministry of 1868–74. He had retired from the leadership of his party, which was divided and embarrassed. Very few of his colleagues had any sympathy with the attitude he adopted, or with the new and unheard-of methods he employed to arouse national feeling. Single-handed, he challenged the long-accepted doctrine, which he had himself earlier upheld, that it was an essential principle of English policy to maintain the strength and integrity of the Turkish empire ; and he challenged it, not on the ground of national interest, but in the name of justice to the oppressed, because he saw in the Turkish rule over the Christians of the Balkans a horror worse even than the iniquities of Bomba. There cannot be much doubt that, but for Gladstone, the England of the 'seventies would have accepted the Turkish atrocities in Bulgaria as placidly as we have accepted those in Armenia. But by the electric power of his eloquence he swung round more than half of the nation to the belief that the accepted policy of a hundred years should be reversed. More than that, he convinced them, for the moment at any rate, that neither national prestige nor national interests should be the supreme criterion of foreign policy, but the establishment of justice and the expansion of liberty.

In this thrilling adventure, Gladstone found himself forced to envisage the whole problem of international policy ; and he was brought to do in this sphere what he was always reluctant to do, and perhaps never did, in any other sphere, not even in finance—he laid down the broad principles of national policy in a form which might be embodied in a party creed or catechism. In a famous speech at West Calder he defined six principles which, though they arose from the controversy of the moment, are as applicable to the conditions of to-day as they were to the circumstances of that time. The first of these principles was that the prime interest of the nation is the maintenance of peace. By this he did not mean merely abstention from war ; Gladstone was no absolute pacifist, but held that some wars, especially wars for liberty, are both just and necessary. He meant active co-operation in the maintenance of peace throughout the world : his first principle was thus positive, not merely negative. The second was that peace can be maintained only by co-operation with other nations, in the concert of Europe. The third was that we ought to avoid all specific alliances or entangling engagements such as we had made with Turkey : our only engagements should be with the whole concert of Powers, not with any section of them. The fourth was that our influence in this co-operation should always be used for the maintenance and extension of liberty. The fifth—inspired, doubtless, by memories of Palmerston—was that we have no right to dictate the course which ought to be pursued, and that any attempt to do so will be apt to endanger the very causes we desire to serve. And the sixth was that in international relations all nations ought to be treated as equals, having an equal right to be considered in matters which concern them—an assertion which directly challenged the accustomed dictatorship of the Five Great Powers.

No one who studies without prejudice this statement of principles can fail to be impressed by the extent to which it anticipates the trend of modern thought on these questions, and the lessons which the armed peace and the Great War have forced upon us. It is, in truth, an anticipation of the international scheme embodied in the League of Nations. Gladstone was, indeed, the greatest prophet of this ideal. " The statesmen of to-day have a new mission opened to them ", he wrote to a French leader in 1866, " the mission of substituting the concert of nations for their conflicts, and of teaching them to grow great in common." And as to the part which England should play in this mission: "This country should seek to develop and mature the action of a common, or public, or European opinion, as the best standing bulwark against wrong", he wrote to General Grey in 1869. "But she should beware of seeming to lay down the law of that opinion by her own authority, and thus running the risk of setting against her, and against right and justice, that general sentiment which ought to be, and generally would be, arrayed in their favour."

All this doctrine is in the sharpest conflict with the doctrine of power, of which Bismarck was the supreme exponent. It conceives of an ideal Europe neither as a group of natural enemies, perpetually suspicious and on the alert to take advantage of one another, nor as a single vast super-state dominated by a single cosmopolitan authority, but as a partnership of free nations working in organised co-operation. It places in a just balance those two complementary principles of national freedom and international co-operation, which are too often treated as if they were mutually incompatible, whereas nationalism and internationalism are, like law and liberty, each imperfect and insecure without the other. Although Gladstone is seldom thought of as having achieved anything in the

sphere of foreign politics, I am inclined to think
that it was here that his political thinking took
the highest and noblest sweep, because here alone
the ardour of his conviction melted that strange
reluctance to commit himself in uncompromising
statements, or to go beyond the immediate practical
necessities, which I have so often noted as a governing factor in his development.

VII

There was one other issue upon which his full
power was expended — the question of Ireland —
which occupied more of his thoughts and effort than
any other.   Except during the period of his conflict
over the Eastern question, it dominated his mind
during the whole of the second and greater half
of his public life, from 1867 to 1894.   Indeed, it
began to master him even earlier.   There is a
striking sudden outburst in a private letter to Mrs.
Gladstone, dating from the turning-point year
1850 : " Ireland, Ireland ! " he breaks out, " that
cloud in the west, that coming storm, the minister
of God's retribution upon cruel and inveterate and
but half-atoned injustice ".   The Irish question
seemed to bring into focus all the emotions which
had been successively stirred in each phase of his
intellectual pilgrimage: his hatred of oppression;
his belief in religious freedom; his sympathy for the

national sentiment; his conviction, supported by colonial experience, that a participation of freedom is the strongest bond of unity between peoples; his slowly achieved belief that liberty rather than authority is the cement of States. In each of his two longest ministries, 1868–74 and 1880–85, his personal interest was concentrated upon Ireland, and the numerous reforms upon which his colleagues were engaged occupied only a secondary place in his attention. In his two later ministries, 1886 and 1892–94, all his powers were almost exclusively devoted to the losing battle for Irish self-government. I need not dwell upon these battles, heroic as they were. This generation, which has conceded to force a degree of self-government vastly greater than Gladstone wished to make as a free concession to justice, must find it difficult to imagine or recall the intensity of that old fight, the last of a fighting career, and the only one in which the warrior had to accept defeat. But to the student of Gladstone's career Ireland presents perhaps the clearest illustration of the slow dawning of conviction upon his mind, and the indomitable courage with which he fought for his conviction once he had attained it.

But there is one aspect of the long Irish struggle which deserves emphasis, because it strikingly illustrates the feature of Gladstone's political thought to which I have so often referred—his freedom from rigid doctrinaire theories, and his

readiness to break away from half-accepted doctrines
when he was brought up against a problem to which
they appeared to be inapplicable.   In his legislation
on Irish land, at two successive stages, Gladstone
boldly broke away from the accepted doctrines of
his time regarding the interference of the State in
economic processes, and tried to use the power of the
State to reconstruct the economic foundations of a
nation's life.   And it is very necessary to remember
this when we consider his attitude towards that
vital aspect of politics on which his contribution
was least—the social problem.

VIII

Upon the whole, it is fair to say that he never
seriously addressed his mind to the social problem ;
never asked himself whether the service of liberty
did not demand that the power of society should
be used to ensure the conditions of good living for
the mass of its members ;   never accepted the
doctrine which, in his later years, T. H. Green was
preaching—the doctrine that the State must not
merely remove obstacles to individual enterprise,
but must create the positive conditions of liberty
which will enable the individual to be the master
of his own powers and to exercise them in freedom.
Upon the whole, he accepted the Manchester
doctrine that the State should not meddle in

economic matters, though, as we have seen, he repudiated the identification of Liberalism with *laissez-faire*. It is true that the ministries of which he was a member were responsible for a large majority of the Factory Acts, which involved an increasing degree of State interference with industrial processes. But though he accepted these measures as necessary, and never adopted the strict doctrinaire attitude which led his friend Bright to oppose them, he never put his mind on to the question, or realised the full significance of these measures. This was not one of the questions upon which he was forced by the teaching of events to examine the foundations of his belief. It is true, again, that the Education Act of 1870 was passed by his ministry. But he accepted it without enthusiasm : popular education was never one of the issues upon which he became a zealot.

At the end of his life he was perturbed and uneasy because he saw that opinion was drifting into a new attitude on these issues, and his breach with Chamberlain was largely due to this uneasiness. " The pet idea of the Liberalism of to-day ", he wrote to Lord Acton in 1885, " is what they call construction—that is to say, taking into the hands of the State the business of the individual. . . . This has much to estrange me, and has had for many years." And to the Duke of Argyll he wrote deploring " the leaning of both parties to Socialism,

which I radically disapprove "—just as, fifty years
earlier, he had radically disapproved the movement
towards religious equality and political democracy.

There are those who think of Gladstone primarily
as an exponent of *laissez-faire* economics, and the
phrases I have just quoted might seem to give
colour to this view. But it is a view which not
only disregards some of his most potent achievements, but forgets that he was less than most
statesmen the slave of formulæ, and more than
most statesmen the teachable pupil of events. I
have already noted the comment of a follower in
1864 that " he does not hesitate to apply the full
power of the State to ameliorate social anomalies " ;
the man of whom this was said had already framed
the Railways Act, which was a far more drastic
method of exercising State control over great
monopolies than anybody has yet dared to suggest
in any other sphere, and had already established
State savings banks and other devices. Later,
when faced with the problem of Irish land, he made
the boldest departure from traditional economic
orthodoxy that had yet been undertaken, setting
up, in place of competition for farms, tenant-right
and the fixation of rents by land-courts.

At the end of his life, engrossed though he was by
Ireland, he was forced to face the land problem in
England also—a problem to which, as he confessed,
he had not hitherto given serious thought ; and in

speeches in 1889 and 1891 he indicated the movement of his thought in a manner that must have startled those who regarded him as the apostle of *laissez-faire*, and might have startled himself if he had remembered his own utterances of a few years earlier. The labourer must be given land, he proclaimed. As a means to that end, the landlord must, where necessary, be expropriated by the State, not for the creation of small properties, which seemed to him impracticable on any large scale, but for the creation of State-tenancies ; and if nationalisation of the land became necessary, it must not be ruled out on merely theoretical grounds.

Here was the announcement of another change of view, brought about by the teaching of events. If Gladstone had been twenty years younger, if his mind had not been engrossed by one dominating question, if it had been free to receive the impact of all those influences which were changing opinion in the last two decades of the nineteenth century— the inquiries of Charles Booth and others into the problem of poverty, the teachings of the London dock strike of 1889, the decadence of rural England, the manifest insecurity of the foundations of life among industrial workers—if, I say, his mind had been as open to new impressions as it was in earlier days, it is surely impossible to assert that his view would not have changed, as it had changed on so many earlier issues.

S

Distrustful as he was of the new temper which he saw growing in influence, he was indeed aware that a new era was opening.   In his farewell address to the electors of Midlothian, on his retirement in 1894, he looked back upon three score years, which he described as a period of great legislative and administrative achievement, and predominantly a period of emancipation.   He recognised that " another period has opened ".   But he did not attempt to characterise it, still less suggest that his successors should stand fast upon the ideas to which his pilgrimage had hitherto led him, or shut their minds to those teachings of events to which he had himself so often submitted.   He was content, on his withdrawal, to remind the people " that their present political elevation is owing to no principles less broad and noble than these—the love of liberty, of liberty for all without distinction of class, creed, or country ; and the resolute preference of the interests of the whole to any interest, be it what it may, of a narrower scope ".

To think of Gladstone as a man of fixed ideas and unchangeable doctrine is indeed the most profound of blunders.   His was a powerful, but never a systematising, intellect, swept forward into unsuspected courses by a profound moral fervour that welled from the depths of his being and was sustained by an intense religious belief.   He could not, perhaps, at any time of his life have set forth his political creed in the clear-cut formulæ in which many men rejoice, and if he had done so, the formulæ would have been falsified by the later teachings of experience. But, from the time when he first gained contact with the responsibilities of statesmanship, one ruling principle took command of his soul, the love of liberty; and he followed its guidance. " I have been a learner all my life ", he said at the end of his career. " I still have some ideas that may not be thought to furnish good materials for a Liberal politician. I do not like changes for their own sake. I have a great reverence for antiquity. The basis of my Liberalism is this. It is a lesson I have been learning ever since I was young. I am a lover of liberty." In his long life that passion led him to many unexpected conclusions. If his life had been twice as long, it would have led him to many more. It led him to no single conclusion upon which he has not in the long run been followed by the opinion of his countrymen.

THE MARQUESS OF SALISBURY

By C. H. K. MARTEN

I

ON the 3rd of February 1830 was born a baby who was destined to become Prime Minister of Great Britain and to control its foreign policy for a very long period. His name was Robert Cecil. He became Lord Cranborne in 1865, Marquess of Salisbury in 1868, and he died in 1903. His political principles are the subject of this lecture. I do not propose to inquire into the political principles of Robert Cecil in his bib and porringer stage of existence ; but I must begin to consider them when he entered Eton at the age of ten, as he held even then political principles which he maintained throughout his life. Public schools were rougher places then than they are now, and I am afraid that Robert Cecil's life at Eton was not a happy one. To a certain extent it was his own fault. He was a thin frail boy, but could not resist the lure of the " sock " or " tuck-shop " ; and we may suspect that not infrequently he ate, with disastrous results, too much. Then he was one of those untidy, unbusinesslike boys who, as his tutor said, lost a hat every forty-eight hours. It was, however, his political principles that got him into trouble with other boys. One of the most marked character- istics of Lord Salisbury throughout his life was, as we shall see later, his individualism. He disliked, by taste and on principle, interference by others with himself, and did not himself like interfering with others. A small boy as a rule, however, is apt to be communistic. He believes in sharing everything, whether it be a cake or a facility for doing Latin verses, especially if it happens to be some one else's cake or some one else's facility. At that time at Eton Latin verses provided the chief exercise of the week. Lord Salisbury was very good at them, and was constantly asked by the other boys for help. But Lord Salisbury objected to sharing this aptitude. "I am ob- noxious to them all", he wrote home at the age of fourteen, "because I can do verses, but I will not do them for the others, not choosing to sacrifice my liberty at the bidding of one lower than myself. They call me stingy because I won't do verses, and take it out in bullying." Lord Salisbury may have been one of those boys who rather exaggerate their own unhappiness ; but at any rate he thought himself unhappy, and persuaded his father to let him leave Eton at the age of fifteen.

At the age of eighteen Lord Salisbury went to Oxford. There by political principle he was an ardent protectionist and an equally ardent believer in absolute government. When he was a small boy at Eton Lord Dufferin remembered his writing " such clever essays " ; and his ability at Oxford was generally recognised. Shrewd judges, his daughter records in her life of Lord Salisbury, thought his opinions would develop and that he would end as a Liberal Prime Minister. It is curious that Macaulay should have called Gladstone —also an Eton and Christ Church man—the rising hope of the " stern and unbending Tories " when he was young, and that the prophets were wrong in both cases.

In 1854, at the age of twenty-four, Lord Salisbury went into Parliament and his public life began. In that same year his father offered him the colonelcy of the Middlesex militia. Salisbury had no love or aptitude for the army, and the offer was received with dismay. " Your proposal gave me a stomach ache ", he wrote to his father, " all the morning. I detest soldiering beyond measure. As far as tastes go I would sooner be at the treadmill." And he went on to say that if he was to be of any use in Parliament all his energies must be used for reading.

Lord Salisbury—or Lord Robert Cecil as he then was—entered Parliament in 1854, and was to remain in public life till he gave up the Prime Ministership in 1902. We will begin by saying something of his political opinions during the fourteen years from 1854–68, during which time he was in the House of Commons.

That period corresponded to the ten years of Lord Palmerston's dictatorship, 1855–65, which was broken only for some fifteen months by the brief ministry of Lord Derby. Then followed, on Lord Palmerston's death in 1865, the three short-lived ministries of Lord Russell, of Lord Derby— during which the Reform Bill of 1867 was passed— and of Benjamin Disraeli.

These years from 1854–68, the years in his life from the age of twenty-four to thirty-eight, are the years during which Lord Salisbury is the critic. He is the critic not only of the opposing party but of his own party as well, and especially of one of the chief figures in it, that of Benjamin Disraeli. Only for one brief spell of nine months was he in office—the rest of the time he was in opposition either to the Whigs or to his own Conservative party. He used to say that during these years in which he was in the House of Commons he was an Ishmaelite—his hand against every man's and every man's hand against his. Certainly during that time he must have been rather a trial to prime ministers and other important people ; and I observe that their references to him in the new instalment of the Queen's Letters are not flattering. "He never loses an opportunity of doing an unhandsome thing ", says Lord Palmerston in one letter ; and Disraeli says in a letter to the Queen in 1865, "He made a very bitter attack on the Ministry. Nothing could be more malignant, but it lacked finish."

During this period there is a great abundance of material for Lord Salisbury's political ideas, and I propose to let Lord Salisbury, so far as possible, state his own opinions in his own words—for no one could express them more trenchantly or more cogently. We have not only his letters and his speeches in the House of Commons and elsewhere, but there are in addition no less than thirty-three articles that he contributed to the *Quarterly Review*, most of which were written during this period. The first article appeared in 1860, when he was thirty years old, and produced something of the same excitement as the first article of Macaulay's did in the *Edinburgh Review*, when he was only twenty-five—though the authorship in Lord Robert Cecil's case was at first unknown.

II

Now what were Salisbury's principles during those fourteen years ? Two things have to be remembered in connection with them. First, that he was earnest and young. There is an interesting letter written by him when he was Secretary of State for India, to the Queen, about a clergyman whom he wanted to make Bishop of Bombay. An objection urged to the appointment was that the clergyman in question was too " rigid ". " Earnest men," says Lord Salisbury, " when young, are almost always rigid. As experience comes the rigidity wears off, but the earnestness remains." And I am inclined to think that this is true of Lord Salisbury himself. Secondly, except for two short intervals, the Conservatives during the whole of these years were in Opposition—and it was, after all, the business of Her Majesty's Opposition to oppose the measures of Her Majesty's Government.

Certainly Lord Salisbury did oppose, and frequently with very ingenious arguments, the Whig and Liberal measures of that time. Take some of the reforms — the substitute, for example, of competitive examinations for nomination in public appointments ; he defined the scheme as " one for the bestowing of appointments not upon persons who were qualified for them but upon those who had shown their fitness for something else ". Then again he was anxious that the connection between the Church of England and the Universities of Oxford and Cambridge should be maintained : if Dissenters were admitted they ought not to be allowed to be members of Convocation and to influence University legislation.

This is the point to which all my fears are directed. I have no wish to deprive Dissenters of any honours which they may gain at the Universities, or to deny them the merited fruit of their learning and labours ; but I maintain that the University of Oxford is intended to teach everything which it is important for a citizen of this country to know ; and of all things it is important for a man to know the first and foremost is religion. I maintain, too, that if they admit Dissenters into the governing body, that most essential part of University education must sooner or later be abandoned.

The three subjects, however, which were dominant during this period were those of finance, foreign policy, and the reform of Parliament. Let us see what the political principles of Lord Robert Cecil were in each of these subjects at this time.

Each year of Lord Palmerston's administration from 1859–65 witnessed the Budget of Gladstone, his Chancellor of the Exchequer ; and the great event of each year was Mr. Gladstone's Budget speech. Gladstone's first great speech in 1860 was made in dramatic circumstances. He had been ill with a bad cold. The wildest rumours were afloat. The Budget had to be postponed from Tuesday to Friday ; and when the House assembled on Friday, members were still doubtful as to whether Gladstone would be able to appear.

I hope you will forgive me for quoting here Lord Salisbury's description of the scene, which, for all its sarcasm, is a fine tribute to Gladstone's genius and an example of Lord Salisbury's vivid style of writing when a young man of thirty.

Undoubtedly such an opportunity for display has seldom fallen to an orator's lot, and has still more seldom been so skilfully improved. The stage effects were so admirably arranged, the circumstances that led up to the great speech were so happily combined that there were not wanting malicious tongues to suggest that that convenient impressive bronchitis was nothing but an ingenious *ruse*. Certainly never was cold timed so opportunely. If it had lasted longer, Sir G. C. Lewis must have brought the Budget forward ; and then the House of Commons would have been unquestionably able to give it a most dispassionate consideration. If it had not come at all, the orator would not have found his audience predisposed in his favour by the high-wrought tension of their expectations, as well as by their sympathy for the heroic will that mastered even a rebellious uvula in the cause of duty. The very doubt that prevailed whether he could do it enhanced the amiability of his audience. Down to the very moment before he began, nay, down to the close of his glorious peroration, criticism and censure were hushed by a feeling of anxious uncertainty as to whether huskiness or heroism would have the mastery at last. . . .

The Treasury Bench grew fuller and fuller ; but no Mr. Gladstone was to be seen. An anxious murmur began to circulate through the excited, expectant House. He was known to have been in bed on Tuesday, and the doctor was said to have talked of congestion on the lungs. Was it possible that he should attempt a Budget speech on the Friday ? At last a general cheer arose, as the long-looked-for orator, with his usual stealthy, almost timid, step, noiselessly slid into his place. A few minutes of other business, and he rose to speak. It was impossible for the most embittered opponent to avoid scanning his features with something of sympathy, or anxiously trying to trace in his tones whether it was possible that sheer determination and mental vigour would really carry him through. His face was pale, and he occasionally leant against the table with an appearance of fatigue, as though standing was an effort; but his tones were as melodious, his play of features and of gesture was as dramatic as ever. Throughout the whole four hours of intricate argument neither voice nor mind faltered for an instant. Of the success of the speech there is no need to tell. Looked at from a distance, there does not seem much in a Chancellor of the Exchequer having a bad cold; but, at the time, this vulgar accessory added marvellously to the effect of what was in itself one of the finest combinations of reasoning and declamation that has ever been heard within the walls of the House of Commons.

But if Lord Robert Cecil could admire the speech and the speaker, he had strong objections to parts of the Budget. The abolition of custom duties was the characteristic of Gladstone's Budgets, and Gladstone had boasted that whereas in 1845 the number of articles subject to customs duties was 1163 and in 1853 460, that number had now been reduced to 40. Lord Robert Cecil's objection to the Budget was that it upset the balance between direct taxation as represented by the Income Tax and indirect taxes as represented by these duties. His ideas are still worth hearing.

Here, for instance, is his reference to the " simplicity " of Gladstone's Budget.

Simplicity was the chief credit which Mr. Gladstone claimed for the customs legislation of the past year. He and his eulogists were accustomed to boast that the tariff had been reduced from 400 to 40 articles ; and they seemed to imagine that when they had made that boast they had established a self-evident claim to the admiration of mankind. The phrase caught the public fancy, and everybody went about talking of the enormous advantages of the " simplification of the tariff ". What those advantages were nobody ever stopped to explain. Some people were satisfied with a dim recollection that they had heard accounts praised for simplicity, and that tariffs and accounts had some sort of connection with each other. Others looked upon tariffs as things to be learnt by heart, and concluded that the tariff which was easiest remembered was sure to be the best. Others recollected their early preference for simple over compound arithmetic, and, impressed by the recollection, instinctively assumed that simplicity must always have a fascination of its own. But all the sufferers under the various tortures applied to them by the Budget agreed to console each other with the remark that the simplification of the tariff was a great thing.

And this is how he deals with the objection that customs duties are a hindrance to commerce.

It is quite true that duties of customs and excise, even the best of them, are in some sort a hindrance to commerce. But the same stigma attaches to every tax that ever was devised. A duty on silk makes silk dear ; and if a man, or a community, can only afford a certain sum to spend in silk, it is obvious enough that less silk will be bought

when the duty is on it than when it is off. To that extent
the industry of all persons engaged in the manufacture,
carriage, and sale of silk will suffer, and of course the
industry of all those whom they in their turn employ.
To that extent the indirect tax hinders trade. But is the
direct tax more innocent ? When men pay Income Tax,
they must save it out of something : they must retrench
somewhere to provide the means of paying. Suppose they
retrench in silk. The silk merchant's trade is in precisely
the same case as if it was subject to a customs duty. The
consumer's power of buying is equally shortened, and the
trade is equally checked, whether the duty be taken out
of his pocket by the collector at his house or by the
tradesman across the counter in the shape of an increased
price. . . . Commercially speaking, therefore, it is all one
whether the revenue be raised out of direct or indirect
taxation, always supposing both to be applied to legitimate
objects in a legitimate way.

In an article written in 1865, though acquies-
cing in some of Gladstone's financial measures,
he questioned the grounds of the self-complacency
of Gladstone and his disciples.

It is natural that men should exaggerate the importance
of the affairs in which they themselves have been concerned and the efforts in which they have borne a part.
Captain Marryat tells us that it was a fixed persuasion
among the Barbadians that the staunchness of Barbadoes
was the one thing which enabled England to brave with
success the perils of the Revolutionary War. Mr. Gladstone
looks upon the energy and the industry of Englishmen
from a point of view very similar to that of the gallant
Barbadians. Englishmen may be deluded enough to think
that if they have multiplied forges and factories, mines
and docks—if they have spread their commerce over every

sea, and filled every market with their industry—if they
have accumulated unexampled wealth—the result is owing
to the happiness of their invention, the boldness of their
enterprise, the tenacity of their perseverance, and the
bounty of Nature, which all these qualities have turned to
the best account. Mr. Gladstone and Lord Russell know
better. It is due to their wisdom in taking off the duty
on corn in 1846, and the duty on soap in 1853, and the duty
on paper in 1861. We are far from contesting the salutary
nature, speaking abstractedly, of these and of some other
similar changes which have taken place in the levy of
customs and excise duties. They have been made
hastily, sometimes with undue partiality to special
interests, and to the neglect of other remissions which had
a preferable claim. But in principle they were sound,
and, so far as they went, have been beneficial in their
operation. But it is ridiculous to suppose that they have
added any appreciable volume to the vast and swelling
stream of English commerce.

Gladstone's Budgets during Lord Palmerston's
second Ministry of 1859–65, in spite of Lord Salisbury's criticisms, have been regarded as a great
achievement ; but the foreign policy during the
same administration of Lord Russell, the Foreign
Secretary, and of Lord Palmerston, the Prime
Minister, those two "dreadful old men", as the
Queen once in a moment of irritation called them,
has found few supporters. To the foreign policy
of these two Lord Salisbury devoted more than
one article in the *Quarterly*. He called it a policy
" which was dashing, exacting, dauntless to the
weak and timid and cringing to the strong ". He

illustrated his criticisms by examining their policy towards two weak States, Brazil and Japan, whom they had bullied for very insufficient reasons, and contrasting it with their policy towards Poland and Denmark when opposed by Russia and the German States and more especially Prussia. With these latter events you are familiar. There had been an insurrection in Poland against Russia, and we had tried to intervene. The only result was that the Poles were encouraged to continue in a hopeless resistance, and then we found we could do nothing because on the Polish question we had against us Russia supported by Prussia. There followed the final humiliation. This I will give in Salisbury's own words.

When the last defiance of Prince Gortchakoff [the Russian minister] had arrived and the Government had made up their minds to practise the better part of valour, Lord Russell made a speech at Blairgowrie, and being somewhat encouraged and cheered by the various circumstances of consolation which are administered by an entertainment of that kind, he recovered after dinner somewhat of his wonted courage, and under the influence of the valour so acquired he proclaimed that, in his opinion, Russia had sacrificed her treaty title to Poland. Having made the statement thus publicly, he felt that he could do no less than insert it into the despatch to Prince Gortchakoff, with which it was proposed to terminate the inglorious correspondence. He flattered himself, indeed, that so hostile an announcement, while not leading actually to a war, might enable him to ride off with something like a flourish, which his friends might construe into a triumph.

And so the despatch was sent off, formally bringing the correspondence to a close, and concluding with the grandiose announcement that, in the opinion of the British Government, Russia had forfeited the title to Poland which she had acquired by the Treaty of Vienna. But even this modest attempt to escape from disgrace was not destined to succeed. When the despatch reached St. Petersburg, it was shown to Prince Gortchakoff before being formally presented. " You had better not present this concluding sentence to me," is reported to have been the Prince's brief but significant observation. The hint was taken; the despatch was sent back to England and submitted anew to the Foreign Secretary. Doubtless with disgust, but bowing to his inexorable destiny, he executed this new act of self-abasement. The offending sentence was erased by its author with the resolution of a Christian martyr. In this form it was sent back to Russia ; and it still bears, as published to the world, in the bald mutilation of the paragraph with which it concludes and in the confusion of its dates, the marks of its enforced and reluctant revision.

Then there was the dispute between Denmark and the German States about Schleswig and Holstein in which we played so inglorious a part, and which finally led to the two provinces being taken by Austria and Prussia, and, after the Prussian war of 1866, annexed by Prussia alone. On this subject Lord Salisbury was very bitter.

Let the reader compare with these promises [that England had made] the scenes that are passing and have passed in Slesvig and Jutland, and the whole tale of England's disloyalty and Denmark's ruin is before him. For years we have thrust ourselves forward as her friends, taken her under our special protection, and proclaimed

T

with tedious iteration in every court in Europe that her integrity and independence are the first object of our care. We have loaded her with good advice, meddled in her smallest concerns, and treated her almost as an English dependency—so keen and so peculiar was the interest we affected to feel in her welfare. Actuated by the hopes— the encouraged hopes—of help in an unequal struggle, she did not resent this intrusion into her affairs. On the contrary, she yielded to our pressure. At our instance she made concession after concession. With each new concession her adversaries—those who coveted her soil—were encouraged to put forward new demands, and with each new demand England urged a new concession. Under the pressure of our urgency, deeply against her own convictions, she abandoned Holstein to their will, and evacuated fortresses which she might have defended, at least for a time. She resigned, perhaps for ever, that splendid prize for which the mightiest nations would be glad to compete, the harbour of Kiel, which her naval superiority might have enabled her to hold even against an overwhelming force. At all events she gave up, at our bidding, without a struggle, territory upon which she might have at least gained a respite, which would have enabled her to mature her own defences, and would have probably raised up for her allies. For all these concessions we gave her—not a formal promise of aid—no! but intimations of our intention to afford it, which at first sight seemed plain and unmistakable, and only when read by the light of events are discovered to have been intentionally and cunningly ambiguous. The crisis at last has come. The concessions upon which England has insisted have proved futile. The independence which she professed to value so highly is at an end. The people whom she affected to befriend are in danger of being swept away. One of the most wanton and unblushing spoliations which history records is on the point of being consummated. But as far as effective aid goes, England stands aloof. Her pledges and her threats are gone with last year's snow, and she is content to watch with cynical philosophy the destruction of those who trusted to the one, and the triumph of those who were wise enough to spurn the other.

I have alluded to these two events because they had a permanent effect on Lord Salisbury's political principles as regards foreign policy.

" The iron ", says his daughter in her admirable biography of her father, " entered deeply into his soul. In the years to come, when he himself was at the Foreign Office, excited patriots or still more excited philanthropists would sometimes clamour to have their feelings vicariously relieved for them—would demand that insulting strength should be met by threats, or oppressed weakness be supported by sympathy, though they shrank from facing the actual alternative of war if the menaces should be disregarded, or the encouragement disastrously acted upon. In announcing his stubborn refusal to yield to such appeals, he would support it by recalling, with a bitterness which time could not assuage, the catastrophe of shame into which a similar indifference to the responsibilities of language had plunged the country at the time of the German conquest of Schleswig-Holstein."

The subject that takes up most space in the *Quarterly Review* articles is that of the Reform of the House of Commons. The Reform Bill of 1832 had given the vote in the boroughs to the £10 householder, and in the counties to those paying a rent of £10 if they were long leaseholders and of £50 rent if they were " tenants at will ". The question now was as to how far the franchise was

to be extended. Between 1852 and 1867 no less
than six Reform Bills were introduced into Parliament by various Ministers. Lord Robert Cecil
himself was not opposed to a Reform Bill extending
the franchise. He was in favour in principle of the
ideal of the "participation" of the working classes
in the Government without their "predominance".
But such a Bill must prevent "any one class dominating over another. No matter what the class,
such is the selfishness of mankind, tyranny is almost
sure to result." Moreover, he held that to combine
democracy or the government of numbers with
government by the best men was an impossibility.
"First-rate men will not canvass mobs: and mobs
will not elect first-rate men". He denied, again,
that freedom and progress were necessary features
of democracy or that the world was permanently
progressing towards democracy. And I think in
view of what is happening now in Spain and Italy
and Russia and what may happen in France his
opinions have a special significance.

There is no obvious ground for assuming that masses
of men are calmer and more free from passion than
individuals. Such an assumption, if not founded in the
nature of things, is certainly not countenanced by
history. The Athenian people were not remarkable for
clemency or self-restraint, and played the tyrant in their
time as bloodily as any Persian or Macedonian king. . . .
The feverish interval during which France enjoyed the
blessings of pure Democracy will not be upheld, even by

the most advanced Liberal, as a period remarkable for the respect that was paid to individual freedom. There is nothing, therefore, in experience, and nothing in theory, to authorise the connection of the two ideas of freedom and Democracy. But it has been done systematically and perseveringly ; and perseverance has been rewarded with the success which generally awaits it. The two have been put together until people have come to believe that they are connected.

The juxtaposition of the ideas of " Progress " and Democracy, which has been established with equal success, has been more curious still. It is more utterly at variance with the teaching of history. It is quite true that the history of the human race has been the record of a continual progress ; but it is not true that that progress has been identified with a movement towards Democracy, or that it has been the most strikingly displayed in countries where that form of government prevailed. For the future it is, of course, impossible to speak ; but, as regards the past, it is a simple matter of fact that the human race have not progressed towards Democracy. During the experience of the living generation there may have been a movement, not intentionally towards Democracy, but towards a larger development of popular power out of which Democracy may possibly grow. But this movement has only been the flow of a tide, whose alternate rise and fall has been recorded ever since the dawn of civilised polity. . . . If there is any lesson which a general survey of history teaches us, it is that the preponderance of power in a State seldom remains in the same hands for any length of time. But the doctrine that all States have been and are intending to entrust this preponderance finally to the multitude is one that cannot be supported by any evidence whatever.

III

It was the Reform question which led to the first great crisis in Lord Salisbury's career. Lord Derby and Disraeli had come into office in 1866, Lord Cranborne—as he then was—accepting office as Secretary of State for India. In the early months of 1867 Disraeli brought forward his scheme for Conservative reform. It included a dual vote for the richer classes, and various what were called " fancy votes "; and it excluded from the franchise the " compound householder ", the person who did not directly pay rates. The Bill in the course of its progress through the House of Commons completely altered its character; all the checks went, and the Bill meant the bestowal of a vote on some millions of new voters.

Opinions differed then and differ now as to Disraeli's conduct in the whole proceeding. Some maintain that it was a great act of political prescience in the course of which Disraeli had to educate his party. But Salisbury at any rate disliked being educated, and to him the whole proceedings were dishonest. He resigned, and in one of the most famous of his articles in the *Quarterly Review*, " The Conservative Surrender ", a number which had to be reprinted no less than seven times, he enunciated his political principles as to party government and showed what a blow Disraeli had dealt at its whole theory.

Our theory of government is that on each side of the House there should be men supporting definite opinions, and that what they have supported in opposition they should adhere to in office ; and that every one should know, from the fact of their being in office, that those particular opinions will be supported. If you reverse that, and declare that, no matter what a man has supported in opposition, the moment he gets into office it shall be open to him to reverse and repudiate it all, you practically destroy the whole basis on which our form of government rests, and you make the House of Commons a mere scrambling place for office.

But however much he disliked the Bill, he accepted the result as irrevocable.

"It is the duty of every Englishman and of every English party ", he wrote, "to accept a political defeat cordially and to lend their best endeavours to secure the success, or to neutralise the evil, of the principles to which they have been forced to succumb. England has committed many mistakes as a nation in the course of her history, but the mischief has been more than corrected by the heartiness with which after each great struggle victors and vanquished have forgotten their former battles and have combined together to lead the new policy to its best results."

The year 1868 saw the entry of Lord Salisbury to the House of Lords, and the same year saw the beginning of the famous Gladstonian administration of 1868 to 1874. Of these years we have no time to say anything. We will only refer to the political views expressed by Lord Salisbury at this time on the subject of the House of Lords. He laid down the functions of the House of Lords in a passage which has become classical.

The object of the existence of a second House of Parliament is to supply the omissions and correct the defects which occur in the proceedings of the first. But it is perfectly true that there may be occasions in our history in which the decision of the House of Commons and the decision of the nation must be taken as practically the same. . . . It may be that the House of Commons in determining the opinion of the nation is wrong, and if there are grounds for entertaining that belief, it is always open to this House, and indeed it is the duty of this House, to insist that the nation shall be consulted, and that one House, without the support of the nation, shall not be allowed to domineer over the other. . . . But when once we have come to the conclusion from all the circumstances of the case that the House of Commons is at one with the nation, it appears to me that—save in some very exceptional cases, save in the highest cases of morality, in those cases in which a man ought not to set his hand to a certain proposition though a revolution should follow from his refusal—it appears to me that the vocation of this House has passed away, and that it must devolve the responsibility upon the nation, and may fairly accept the conclusion at which the nation has arrived.

With regard to the composition of the House of Lords he was very anxious to introduce a certain number of life peers in order to get a greater variety of interests represented. The lawyers had decided—quite wrongly, so many historians think—that the Queen could not create life peers;

and Lord Salisbury was anxious that this power should be granted or restored. He reverted to this scheme in later years, though nothing eventually came of it.

" We belong ", he said, " too much to one class, and the consequence is that with respect to a large number of questions we are all too much of one mind. Now, that is a fact which appears to me to be injurious to the character of the House as a political assembly in two ways. The House of Lords, though not an elective, is strictly a representative assembly, and it does, in point of fact, represent very large classes in the country. But if you wish this representation to be effective, you must take care that it is sufficiently wide ; and it is undoubtedly true that, for one reason or another, those classes whose wealth and power depend on commerce and mercantile industry do not find their representation in this House so large or so adequate as do those whose wealth and power depend upon the agricultural interest and landed property. . . . We want, if possible, more representatives of diverse views and more antagonism. On certain subjects, it is true, we have antagonism enough—on Church subjects, for instance, and on the interesting question as to who should occupy the benches opposite. But there are a vast number of social questions deeply interesting to the people of this country, especially questions having reference to the health and moral condition of the people—and on which many members of your Lordships' House are capable of throwing great light, and yet these subjects are not closely investigated here because the fighting power is wanting and the debates cannot be sustained."

IV

We now come to the later part of Lord Salisbury's career, that from 1874 to 1902. From 1854–74, during the first twenty years of his public life, he had had under a year of office; of the last twenty-eight years he was to be in office for nearly twenty. From 1874–78 he was Secretary for India ; from 1878–80 he was Foreign Secretary ; in 1885 and from 1886 to 1892 and from 1895 to 1902 he was Prime Minister, and for most of that time Foreign Secretary as well.

Here perhaps something may be said as to Lord Salisbury's characteristics, as they throw light on his political principles. One was, I think, that he was self-contained and self-dependent. There are some people who can delegate work, who rejoice in a staff of co-workers, who like best to come to a decision by " talking over things " with other people. Lord Salisbury was not one of them. His daughter relates how one day he asked one of his sons whether, when occupied with some matter, he found any advantage in talking it over with a friend, and how surprised he was when the answer was in the affirmative. Lord Salisbury, his daughter says, preferred to consult the sources of information himself, to select his own facts, to arrive at his own conclusions, and then to state them in his own language. I am told, I know not with what truth, that Ministers sometimes nowadays have their speeches made up for them in their departments; and that one department had its speech "torn over" seventeen times before it arrived in a state which was agreeable to the Minister concerned. Such a course would have been abhorrent to Lord Salisbury. When he had to make a speech, he generally had it "in his mind" for some days beforehand and then spoke with no notes at all. The late Lord Curzon recalled one occasion when Lord Salisbury made an important election speech of nearly two hours with only one note in his hand—and that an extract from a speech by Joseph Chamberlain.

I imagine that his policy in any office which he held was very much his own, and that, as Disraeli once said, he "acted for himself". When anything important had to be done he shut himself up in his room which had double padded doors : he locked the outside one, and inside the inner one nothing could be heard, and then he felt himself free. When he was responsible for Foreign Affairs he never went down to the Foreign Office till after lunch, doing the work of the office in his own study in Arlington Street. He did his own work and left the officials of the Foreign Office to carry out theirs—for that was the corollary of his dislike of collaboration. "Never jog a man's elbow when he is holding the reins " was, we are told, a favourite motto of his. Indeed a belief in letting men alone to develop their own thoughts and characters was at the heart of his creed. Alike in his relations with his children and his colleagues he showed this intense dislike of interfering with others. It may be regarded as a failing in that he did not attempt to supervise the work of other departments in the way, for instance, that Peel did—though probably the growth of Governmental work made that any way an impossibility. It is perhaps this immersion in his own work that prevented his taking a very active interest in the personalities of his colleagues. His daughter tells the story of a breakfast party at which Lord Salisbury was present. He sat on the right hand of his host, and asked him in the course of the meal in an undertone who was the man on his host's left. It was W. H. Smith, who had been his colleague for many years, and who was at the time the second man in his Ministry.

Another characteristic of Lord Salisbury was, as Lord Rosebery has pointed out, his scorn of wealth and honours. I am not quite sure that, if I were the owner of Hatfield, I should feel I wanted any more ! But, at any rate, the only honour he would take was the Garter, and that with some considerable reluctance. And always with this went his horror of anything like advertisement, and his dislike of the publicity in which inevitably public men must live. He hated dressing up, and had a particular dislike to silk stockings because they were cold. The story is well known of how for some Court function he put on the uniform of an Elder Brother of Trinity House—his favourite or at any rate least disliked uniform—how he saw a couple of epaulettes lying by and pinned them on. He then came into the presence of King Edward—at that time Prince of Wales—who was a very great expert in such things and was horrified to find that the epaulettes were entirely wrong and belonged to a different uniform altogether. Lord Randolph Churchill once described Mr. Gladstone as the greatest living master of the art of self-advertisement : " Holloway, Colman, and Horniman are nothing compared to him ". He could not have said that of Lord Salisbury. There is a story told of how he went up to Balmoral to see the Queen when the country was in a great state of political excitement. The train had to go through Edinburgh. Lord Salisbury went into the saloon reserved for him at King's Cross, but passed on to a second-class compartment at the end of the carriage and put his valet in the saloon. At Edinburgh station there was a great crowd of reporters and other people who rushed to the windows and gazed bewilderedly at the valet, wondering who he was, while Lord Salisbury watched them complacently from the retirement of his second-class compartment.

Another characteristic of Lord Salisbury was that he was a country gentleman. It is true that for hunting and shooting he did not care; but his interests nevertheless were those of a country gentleman. He was Chairman of Quarter Sessions for twenty years. When he had the time, he took a keen interest in his estates. In 1879 when the agricultural depression came, some of his farmers gave up their farms and Lord Salisbury took them in hand himself. He took great interest in them and used to make up the profit and loss account not only on each farm but also on each field with great care. As is the case with all country gentlemen, his farms never paid; but like all country gentlemen he had an invincible optimism—which no experience could shake—that eventually they would. He was a great builder of cottages on his estates, but he believed in getting an economic rent for them, for otherwise it was unfair on the competing builder. In all, he built no less than 200. These cottages he would not have tied to any farm, but kept the control of them in his own agent's hands, so that the tenants should retain their independence. Lord Salisbury was therefore a practical country gentleman. And he had, as his daughter says, the squire's view of things. The squire's view made him distrust the teaching

of theory or of mere book-learnedness. For instance, on the subject of Free Trade he refused to
dogmatise in later life : though he held that if
we had duties on some articles it would give us
something to bargain with in negotiations with
foreign countries. Again, he distrusted the views
of experts. Of military experts he had a special
distrust. " I think ", he wrote to Lord Lytton in
1877, " you listen too much to the soldiers. No
lesson seems to be so deeply inculcated by the
experience of life as that you never should trust
experts. If you believe the doctors, nothing is
wholesome : if you believe the theologians, nothing
is innocent : if you believe the soldiers, nothing is
safe. They all require to have their strong wine
diluted by a very large admixture of insipid
common sense." At a later period, when there
was a question of giving up to Turkey some forts
garrisoned by Egyptian troops on the coast of
Midian, Lord Salisbury wrote to Lord Cromer :
" I would not be too much impressed by what
the soldiers tell you about the strategic importance of these places. It is their way. If they
were allowed full scope, they would insist on the
importance of garrisoning the Moon in order to
protect us from Mars."

There is one other characteristic which ought
not to be omitted, for it is the underlying factor of
his life—and that was his strong religious sense.

Lord Salisbury used to say that all the men he met who had moved in great affairs had a sense of the supernatural. Lord Salisbury's own belief in Christianity was held, so his daughter says, with all the simplicity of childhood. Every Sunday at Hatfield he had Communion at nine, and went to the Parish Church at eleven, no matter how deeply he was immersed in State affairs. And I remember one instance of his wish to help others in their religion. A clergyman in the south of England had a parishioner who was in great doubt about the Christian religion. The only thing that would satisfy him was, he said, a letter from the Prime Minister. The clergyman wrote to Lord Salisbury, who wrote back giving, for the help of this parishioner, some ten or twelve sides of letter paper regarding his personal convictions. " Personal religion ", says one of his sons, " was the mainspring of his life and the foundation on which all else was built."

V

Now what are we to say of Lord Salisbury's political ideas during this period from 1878 to 1902 ? We have much less to go on. For in a way the era beyond the year 1878 is still closed to us. The Life of Lord Salisbury by his daughter at present goes no further than 1878. The Queen's

Letters stop then also, and the Foreign Office Papers after that date are not available. Moreover persons holding high office, and especially Foreign Secretaries and Prime Ministers, have to be very discreet in what they say or write. Fortunately for the historian this is not altogether true of Lord Salisbury, who was capable of " blazing indiscretions ". But his utterances naturally lost the happy irresponsibility and independence in which he could indulge in opposition and became in a sense less interesting.

In Home Affairs Salisbury was, as we all know, against Home Rule for Ireland. He believed that under it the Loyalists would be sacrificed, and his ideal for Ireland was twenty years of resolute government. Moreover he did not believe that any legislation would lead to the millennium. But he was in favour of easing the shoe where it pinched, and several laws were passed with that object during his Ministry. In particular he was interested in Housing. He was member of a Housing Committee, and steered through the House of Lords the Housing Bill of 1888, which gave the sanitary authorities power of inspection over tenement houses, and which made a man liable for letting unhealthy houses, and gave the Local Government Board power to order local authorities to clear away slums. In the second reading he said :

U

I feel that the condition of the lowest and poorest of the working classes in the most crowded parts of the community is one which, more than any other, deserves attention both outside and in both Houses of Parliament ; because it is by the character of the English race, and the nature of those produced from generation to generation, that you carry on the traditions of the country, fill its armies, perform its public services, and maintain its prosperity, and uphold its ancient reputation ; and their fitness for this must depend upon the physical causes which attend their birth and nurture. Among those physical causes none is more powerful, or more prominent, than the condition of the houses in which they and their parents dwell, and therefore there is none that deserves more earnest, careful, unflagging, and yet circumspect, attention both of the philanthropist and the statesman.

The only other matter in Home Politics I should like to mention is Lord Salisbury's attitude to Reform. To the onward march of democracy he made no further resistance. He was, perhaps, somewhat sceptical as to the value of Parish Councils—he said that people would rather go to a circus than to a parish meeting. In the Reform and Redistribution Bill of 1884 he, however, took a leading part : it was he who went with Stafford Northcote to tea with Gladstone in No. 10 Downing Street, and there the question was settled. Rather curiously Gladstone was startled by Lord Salisbury being " entirely devoid of respect for tradition ", whilst Lord Salisbury was amused by Gladstone's Conservatism. One sentence of Gladstone's was quoted by Lord Salisbury to Lord Carnarvon. Gladstone was referring to the Liberal legislation of the last fifty years and said, " It is very remarkable, so remarkable that it now *left nothing to be done* ! "

VI

I have left to the last the most important part of Lord Salisbury's premiership, his Foreign Policy. For his two years as Foreign Secretary, from 1878–1880, years which included the Treaty of Berlin, we have a large amount of material. For the rest, from 1885, we have the German account from the German archives so far as it affected Germany. But we have no authoritative and detailed account, and for this we must wait for the remaining volumes of Lord Salisbury's biography.

What were Lord Salisbury's political principles in foreign policy ? They were expressed in general terms long before he became Foreign Secretary. " In our foreign policy ", he said at Stamford in 1865, " what we have to do is simply to perform our own part with honour ; to abstain from a meddling diplomacy ; to uphold England's honour steadily and fearlessly, and always to be rather prone to let action go along with words than to let it lag behind them." Five years before in the *Quarterly Review* of April 1860 he had approved (in contrast to the then existing foreign policy of

Palmerston and Canning) the "traditional" part which England had played in Europe—"England did not meddle with other nations' doings when they concerned her not. But she recognised the necessity of an equilibrium and the value of a public law among the states of Europe. When a great Power abused its superiority by encroaching on the frontier of its weaker neighbours, she looked on their cause as her cause and on their danger as the forerunner of her own."

The first subject that Lord Salisbury had to deal with in the years 1878–80 was of course "The Eastern Question". The events are familiar. There had been an insurrection against the Turks in Bulgaria. It was put down by the Turks with characteristic brutality, which caused Gladstone to come out of his retirement and to advocate the "Bag and Baggage" policy with regard to Turkey. A Conference of the Great Powers was held at Constantinople. Lord Salisbury was our representative and an attempt was made to force some scheme of reform on the Turks. But the Turks refused. "Convincing the Turk", said Lord Salisbury, "is about as easy a matter as making a donkey canter." The Conference failed. Russia went to war, marched almost within sight of Constantinople and imposed upon Turkey the Peace of San Stephano. Up to this point Lord Salisbury had supported the peace party in the

Cabinet. But, with Russia threatening our interests in the Near East, he advocated action and the Fleet was sent up the Dardanelles to Constantinople. Lord Derby accordingly resigned and Lord Salisbury became Foreign Secretary.

On the evening after his appointment, after going out to dinner, he sat down at 11 o'clock in his study, and by 3 A.M. the next morning had penned a circular note to the Powers, a note which in Lord Rosebery's opinion achieved for him a European reputation. It is one of the historical State papers of the English language. In it Lord Salisbury did not deny that large changes must be made in south-eastern Europe—indeed they were made by the subsequent Treaty of Berlin. But he did attack, and in most convincing fashion, the articles of the particular treaty which Russia had made ; and asserted in emphatic language the right of other Powers to consider articles in the new treaty which were a modification of existing treaty engagements and inconsistent with them.

The effects of this circular on Europe were profound. Perhaps I may quote a vivacious feminine opinion, that of Queen Victoria's eldest daughter, the Crown Princess of Prussia. She had written in January to deplore the " weak, bungling, and vacillating policy of England " with Lord Derby as Foreign Secretary. " I am perpetually in a pugilistic state of mind as I have to read and

hear so much which is hardly bearable." And
then she wrote in April :

Since Lord Salisbury's Circular one can hold up one's
head again. Now we know that England *has* a policy,
and that it is a clear and right one, and this has already
changed the aspect of the whole question. Except amongst
the sworn friends of Russia, I think there is universal
approval of England's step and England's views, and
everywhere a feeling of relief that at last England should
have come forward and spoken up.

The sequel is well known. The Powers met at
Berlin with Beaconsfield and Salisbury as our
representatives and the Treaty of Berlin was
drawn up. It proved to be no more permanent
than other treaties dealing with the Balkans. But
that it was the best treaty that could have been
made at that time is, I think, a tenable proposition.
Lord Salisbury, however, was not enamoured
of the Turks. Everybody knows his dictum about
England puting her money on the wrong horse in
the Crimean War. Even as early as 1877 he seems
to have contemplated some sort of partition of the
Turkish dominions, and he returned to the project
in later times. But nothing definite came of it.
For without the consent of the other Powers he
could do nothing, and the Council of Powers was
" as slow as a steam roller ". The Armenian
massacres of 1894 and 1896 stirred his passions,
but without the other governments action was

impossible. His only success was in the separation
of Crete from the Turkish Empire. In a despatch
of October 1896 he gave his final opinion as to the
Turks :

" In protecting ", he said, " the Turkish Empire from
dissolution, the Powers had been inspired by the hope that
the many evils by which Ottoman rule was accompanied
would be removed or mitigated by the reforming efforts
of the Government. Not only has this hope been entirely
disappointed, but it has become evident that, unless these
great evils can be abated, the forbearance of the Powers
of Europe will be unable to protract the existence of a
dominion which by its own vices is crumbling into ruin ! '

The great object of Lord Salisbury's foreign
policy from 1886–92, and from 1895–1902, when
he was Prime Minister and Foreign Secretary, was
the preservation of peace. " Our allies are those
who wish to maintain the territorial distribution
as it is without risking the fearful danger of the
terrible arbitrament of war. Our allies are those
who desire peace and goodwill." It is impossible
in this lecture to go in detail into the tangled
history of Foreign Politics between 1886 and 1892
and 1895 and 1902. There were many difficulties
between Great Britain and other countries, chiefly
over the world ambitions of the different European
states. Lord Salisbury, by a policy of what he
himself called " graceful concessions ", made a large
number of arrangements to settle the rival claims.
Of these concessions the one that caused the

greatest controversy was that of Heligoland. Lord Salisbury was very careful, when he thought he had made a good bargain, not to proclaim it. Once when he heard that one of his treaties had been published in the *Standard* he said, " I hope there will be no trumpeting about it ". The most serious, of course, of all the crises that arose was the Fashoda affair with France, when Lord Salisbury took a very strong line and the French had to withdraw. It is clear from the German accounts which have been published that Lord Salisbury gave the impression abroad that he was ready to go to any lengths with France over this question. Then there were difficulties with the United States over Venezuela, and further difficulty over Eastern rivalries in the Far East. Over and above all these was the chronic difficulty that arose over the British occupation of Egypt. And, finally, there was the great hostility shown to England by other European nations at the time of the Boer War.

Meanwhile on the Continent had come the building up of the Triple Alliance of Germany, Austria, and Italy which was completed in 1882, and of the Dual Alliance of France and Russia which was completed in 1893. The hostility of France towards Great Britain drew Great Britain naturally towards the Triple Alliance. Germany was extremely anxious to bring England within

her orbit, and there were two occasions on which
an alliance was suggested. One was in 1879, just
after the Treaty of Berlin, when the German
Ambassador suddenly arrived at Hughenden, the
home of Disraeli, with a suggestion of an alliance.
The Ambassador subsequently saw Lord Salisbury,
but the Germans then seemed to have receded and
nothing came of it. " We are well out of it ", was
Queen Victoria's comment.

It is often said that Lord Salisbury's political
principle in his foreign policy for Great Britain was
one of " splendid isolation ". That is not quite
true, for he did in 1887 have a secret understanding
with Austria and Italy to maintain the *status quo*
in the Eastern Mediterranean. In the same year
came the second offer from Prince Bismarck to
make an alliance between Great Britain and
Germany. Prince Bismarck wrote to the German
Ambassador in London asking him to express to
Lord Salisbury his conviction that the peace which
both England and Germany equally desire cannot
be more surely secured than by the conclusion of
a treaty between Germany and England by which
for a stated time both Powers bind themselves to
mutual protection in the event of a French attack
on either. A *secret* treaty of that nature, if it were
possible, would ensure both Powers increased
security as to the result of such a war, but the
prevention of such a war could only be expected by

the *publication* of the alliance. Salisbury's answer
to this, according to Herbert Bismarck, who was
sent as special Minister, was that though such a
treaty would be the soundest for the peace of Europe
the time was inopportune and that it would lead
to the overthrow of the Government in England.
" Unfortunately ", Lord Salisbury is stated to have
said, " we no longer live in the time of Pitt, when
the Aristocracy ruled and we could pursue an
active policy which made England after the Vienna
Congress the richest and most respected power in
Europe. Now Democracy governs, and with it the
personal and party government which makes every
English government dependent on the *aura popu-
laris*. This generation can only be taught by
events." " Meanwhile," he added, " we leave the
proposal on the table without saying Yes or No ;
that is unfortunately all I can do at present."

After the Emperor William came to the throne,
and Bismarck had retired, a change seemed to
come over the relationship between Great Britain
and Germany. Germany apparently wanted to
drive England out of her policy of isolation, and by
making things difficult for her to compel her to join
the Triple Alliance ; and the Kruger telegram of
1896, of course, aroused a great deal of feeling in
England. But at the close of the Boer War Mr.
Joseph Chamberlain, then Colonial Secretary, seems
to have taken a prominent part in asking Germany

for an alliance, though the whole of the episode is
still rather obscure. There is enough evidence,
however, to show that, so far as Lord Salisbury
himself was concerned, he had become impressed,
at the close of his life, with the falseness of German
policy, and that he did not look with favour on a
closer connection.

But it is time to bring these desultory remarks
to an end. For the full record of Lord Salisbury's
activities we must wait, as I have said, for the
completion of his biography. I will only say this
in conclusion. Lord Rosebery once said of Lord
Salisbury that he was an able, loyal, untiring
servant of his Sovereign and his country ; a public
servant of the Elizabethan style, a fit representative of his great Elizabethan ancestor, Lord Burleigh. And the parallel of the lives of Lord Burleigh
and Lord Salisbury is very close. Lord Burleigh
was born in 1520, Lord Salisbury in 1830. Lord
Burleigh entered the House of Commons as member
for Stamford in 1547, when he was twenty-seven
years old ; Lord Salisbury entered the House of
Commons in 1854, when he was twenty-four years
old, also as member for Stamford. The one died
in 1598, after fifty-one years of public service, and
the other in 1902 after forty-eight years. They
were both voluminous correspondents. They both
served Queens. They were both untiring in their
devotion to the State, and they both spoke their

mind to their rulers, in one case to Queen Elizabeth, and in the other to the British nation. What Queen Elizabeth said to Lord Burleigh when she took him into her service, the British people might have said to Lord Salisbury : " This judgment I have of you that you will not be corrupted with any manner of gifts and that you will be faithful to the State : and that without respect to any private will you will give me that counsel that you think best ". And what finer judgment upon himself could a statesman wish ?

THE END